Themes	Importance
Beginnings	Genesis teaches us that the world is well made and good. People are special to God and unique. God creates and sustains all life.
Disobedience	Genesis explains why people are evil: They chose to do wrong. Even the great Bible heroes failed and disobeyed God.
Sin	Sin ruins people's lives. It happens when we disobey God. Living God's way makes life productive and fulfilling.
Promises	God makes some promises to help and protect people, which is called a "covenant." God kept his promises then, and he keeps them now.
Obedience	Obeying God restores our relationship with him.
Prosperity	Prosperity is deeper than material wealth. True prosperity and fulfillment come as a result of obeying God.

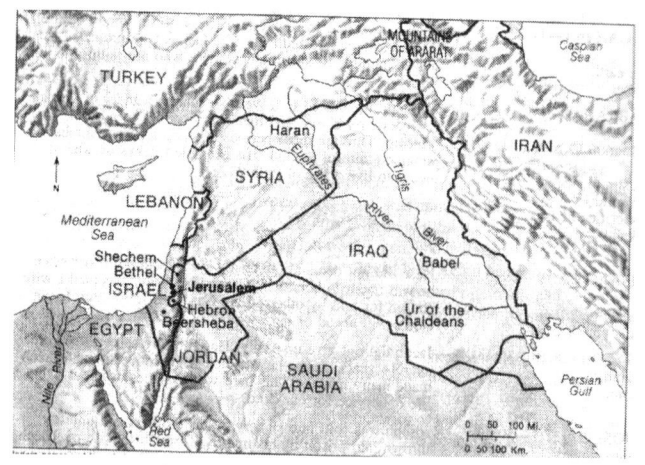

KEY PLACES IN GENESIS

Mountain of Ararat:

Adam and Eve's sin brought sin to the human race. Yes, later it ran rampant and God destroyed the earth by flood, but saved Noah, his family, and 2 of every kind of animal. The ark rested on Mount Ararat (8:4).

Babel:

Again, sin abound and pride of the people led them to build a tower to God. God scattered them and changed their language (11:8,9).

Ur of the Chaldees:

Abram (descendant of Shem & father of the Hebrew nation) was born here (11:27,28).

Haran:

Terah, Lot, Abraham, and Sarah left Ur and followed the Euphrates River, headed toward Canaan. Along the way, they settled in Haran (11:31).

Shechem:

God urged Abraham to leave Haran and go to a place where he would be the father of a great nation (12:1,2). So, Abraham, Lot, and Sarah traveled to the land of Canaan. They settled near Shechem (12:6).

Hebron:

Abraham moved on to Hebron, where he put down his deepest roots (13:18). Abraham, Isaac, and Jacob all lived and was buried here.

Beer-sheba:

A well was dug here as a sign of an oath between Abraham and the army of the King Abimelech (21:3). Years later Isaac was going place to place. God appeared to him and passed onto him the covenant he made with his father, Abraham (26:23—25).

Bethel:

After deceiving his brother, Jacob left Beer-sheba and fled to Haran. Along the way, God appeared in a dream, and passed on the Covenant he had with Abraham and Issac (28:10—22). Jacob lived in Haran, while working for Laban (29:15—30). After meeting with his brother, Jacob returned to Bethel (35:1).

Egypt:

Jacob had 12 sons, including Joseph. His brothers were jealous that Joseph was the favorite. His brothers sold him to Ishmaelite traders, who were going to Egypt. Eventually Joseph rose from Egyptian slave to Pharaoh's--right hand man, saving Egypt and the surrounding country from famine. His family moved from Canaan to Egypt and settled there (46:3—7).

The Blueprint of Genesis:

- Story of Creation ....(1:1—2:3)
- The Story of Adam ....(2:4—5:32)
- The Story of Noah ....(6:1—11:32)
- The Story of Abraham..(12:1—25:18)
- The Story of Issac ....(25:19—28:9)
- The Story of Jacob ....(28:10—36:43)
- The Story of Joseph...(37:1—50:26)

ADAM

We can hardly imagine what it must have been like to be the 1st and only person on earth. This wasn't long, before God, presented him with an Ideal companion and mate, Eve. Theirs was a complete, innocent, and open oneness, without a hint of shame.

Before God made Eve, he had already given Adam complete freedom in the garden, with the responsibility to tend and care for it. But one tree was off-limits, the tree of the knowledge of good and evil. Adam would have told Eve about this. She knew when Satan approached her that the tree's fruit was not to be eaten. However, she decided to eat the fruit, then she offered some to Adam. At that moment, the fate of creation was on the line. Sadly, Adam did not pause to consider the consequences, but went ahead and ate. Because they were one flesh, he was not willing to be separated from his wife. Because Adam loved his wife so much, he was willing to die, separated from God with her.

In that moment of small rebellion something large, beautiful, and free was shattered ... God's perfect creation. Man was separated from God by his desire to act on his own. The effect on a plate of glass window is the same whether a pebble or a boulder is thrown at it—the 1,000's of fragments can never be regathered.

In the case of man's sin, however, God already had a plan in motion to overcome the effects of the rebellion. The entire Bible is the story of how that plan unfolds, ultimately leading to God's own visit to earth through his Son, Jesus Christ. Our small and large acts of rebellion prove that we are descendant of Adam. Only by asking forgiveness from Jesus Christ can we become children of God.

Adam's Strengths and Accomplishments

- 1st zoologist and named of the animals.
- 1st landscape architect.
- Father of the human race.
- 1st made in the image of God and 1st person to share an intimate relationship with God.

Adam's Weaknesses and Mistakes

- Avoided responsibility and blamed others; chose to hide rather than confront; made excuses rather than admitting the truth.
- GREATEST MISTAKE: teamed up with Eve to bring sin into the world.

Lessons from Adam's life

- God wants people who, though free to do wrong, choose instead to love him.
- Don't blame others for their faults and don't hide from God.

Vital Statistics

- WHERE: Garden of Eden
- OCCUPATION: Caretaker, gardener, and farmer
- RELATIVES: Wife → Eve
  Sons → Cain, Abel, Shem, and numerous other children.
  -- He was the only man who had no earthly parents.

EVE

We know very little about Eve, the 1st woman in the world, yet she is the mother of us all. She was the final piece in the intricate and amazing puzzle of God's creation. Here is someone alike enough for companionship, yet different enough for relationship. Together they were greater than either could have been alone

    Satan questioned her contentment. How could she be happy when she was not allowed to eat from one of the fruit trees? Satan helped Eve shift her focus from all that God had done and give them, to the one thing he withheld. Eve was willing to accept Satan's viewpoint without checking with God.

    Does this sound familiar? How often is our attention drawn from the much, which is ours, to the little that isn't? Our desires, like Eve's can be quite easily manipulated. We need to always keep God in our decision-making process. His Word, the Bible, is our guidebook in decision making.

Eve's Strengths and Accomplishments

- 1st wife and mother.
- 1st female. Shared a special relationship with God. Co-responsibility with Adam over creation, and displayed certain characteristics of God.

Eve's Weaknesses and Mistakes

- Allowed her contentment to be undermined by Satan.
- Acted impulsively without talking to God or her husband.
- Sinned and shared her sin with Adam.
- When confronted blamed others.

Lessons from Eve's Life

- The female shares in the image of God.
- The necessary ingredients for a strong marriage are—(Gen 2:24,25)
    - Commitment to each other
    - Companionship with each other.
    - Complete oneness.
    - Absence of shame.
- The basic human tendency to sin goes back to the beginning of the human race.

Vital Statistics

- WHERE: Garden of Eden
- OCCUPATION: Wife, helper, companion, so-manager of Eden
- RELATIVES: Husband➔ Adam
  Sons➔ Cain, Abel, Seth, and numerous other children

ABEL

Abel was the 2nd child born into the world, but the 1st to obey God. His parents were Adam and Eve and he was a shepherd, who presented pleasing sacrifices to God. Abel died at the hands of his jealous older brother, Cain.

Both Cain and Abel knew what God expected, but only Abel obeyed. Throughout history, Able is remembered for his obedience in faith (Hebrews 11:4) and is called "righteous" (Matthew 23:35).

Like Abel, we must obey regardless of the cost, and trust God to make things right.

Abel's Strengths and Accomplishments

- 1st member of the Hall of Faith in Hebrews 11.
- 1st shepherd and 1st martyr for truth Matthew 23:35.

Lessons from Abel's Life

- God hears those who come to him.
- God recognizes he innocent person, sooner or later, punishes the guilty.

Vital Statistics

- WHERE: Just outside of Eden
- OCCUPATION: Shepherd
- RELATIVES: Parents ➔ Adam and Eve
  Brother ➔ Cain

CAIN

Conflicts between children in a family seem inevitable. Sibling relationships allow both competition and cooperation. In most cases, the mixture if loving and fighting eventually creates a strong bond between brothers and sisters. In Cain's case, the troubling potential became a tragedy. Cain got angry and furious. Both he and his brother Abel had made sacrifices to God and his had been rejected. Cain's reaction gives us an idea that his attitude was probably wrong from the start. Cain had a choice to make. He could correct his attitude about his sacrifice to God, or he could take out his anger on his brother, due to jealousy. We may not be choosing to murder, but we are still intentionally choosing what we shouldn't.

    The feelings motivating our behavior can't always be changed by a simple thought-power, but here we can experience God's willingness to help. Asking for his help to do what is right can prevent is from doing what we will regret later.

Cain's Strengths and Accomplishments

- 1st human child and 1st to follow on father's profession of farming.

Cain's Weaknesses and Mistakes

- When disappointed he reacted in anger. Took negative option when the positive was offered. He was the 1st murderer.

Lessons from Cain's Life

- Actions motivated by anger can be sinful. Consequences of sin may last a lifetime. We offer to God from our heart

Vital Statistics

- WHERE: near Eden, probably Iraq or Iran
- OCCUPATION: Farmer and then a nomad
- RELATIVES: Parents➔ Adam and Eve
    - Brothers➔ Abel, Seth, and others not mentioned by name.

THE STORY OF CREATION (1:1—2:3)

We sometimes wonder how our world came to be. But here we find the answer. God created the earth and everything in it, and made man like himself. Although we may not understand the complexity of just how he did it, it is clear that God did create all life. This shows not only God's authority over humanity, but his deep love for all people.

(1:1) ... To say that the universe "just happened" requires more faith than to believe God is behind these amazing statistics. God did not need to create the universe; he chose to create it. Why? God is love and the love is best expressed toward something or someone else-so God created the world and people as an expression of his love. Don't reduce God's creation to merely scientific terms and forget that God created the universe because he loves us. We will never know all the answers to how God created the world, but the Bible tells us that God did create it. That face alone gives worth and dignity to all people.

- (Isa 42:5) ... Thus, saith God the LORD, he that created the heavens, and stretched them out; he that spread forth the earth, and that which cometh out of it; he that giveth breath unto the people upon it, and spirit to them that walk therein:

(1:2) ... Who created God? To ask that question, we have to assume there was another creator before God. At some time, however, we are forced to stop asking that question and realize that there had to be something which has always existed.

(1:3) ... How long did it take God to create the world? There are 2 basic views:
- Each day as a literal 24-hour period.
- Each day represented an indefinite period of time (even 1 million years).
    - → (Ps 33:9) ... For he spake, and it was done; he commanded, and it stood fast.
    - → (2 Cor 4:6) ... For God, who commanded the light to shine out of darkness, hath shined in our hearts, to give the light of the knowledge of the glory of God in the face of Jesus Christ.

Day 2

(Prov 8:28) ... When he established the clouds above: when he strengthened the fountains of the deep:

(Prov 8:29) ... When he gave to the sea his decree, that the waters should not pass his commandment: when he appointed the foundations of the earth:

(Jer 33:25) ... Thus, saith the LORD; If my covenant be not with day and night, and if I have not appointed the ordinances of heaven and earth;

(Ps 104:25—28) ... So is this great and wide sea, wherein are things creeping innumerable, both small and great beasts. There go the ships: there is that leviathan, whom thou hast made to play therein. These wait all upon thee; that thou mayest give them their meat in due season. That thou givest them they gather: thou openest thine hand, they are filled with good.

(1:25) ... Just as God was pleased with his work, we can be pleased with ours. However, we cannot be pleased with our work if God would not be pleased with it. What are you doing that pleases both you and God?

(1:31) ... We were created not as an exact physical sense, instead, we are a reflection of God's glory. Our best hope is to reflect his character in our love, patience, forgiveness, kindness, and faithfulness. Our self-worth comes from being made in his image. If you feel worthless or of little value, remember that God made you for a good reason. You are valuable to him.

(2:2,3) ... We live in an action-oriented world! Yet God demonstrated that rest is appropriated and right. Our times of rest refresh us for times of service.

THE STORY OF ADAM ... (2:4—5:32)

(2:7) ... The body is a lifeless shell until God brings it alive with the "breath of life." Our life and worth come from God's spirit. Value life as he does.

- → (Job 33:4) ... The Spirit of God hath made me, and the breath of the Almighty hath given me life.
- → (Eze 37:5) ... Thus, saith the Lord GOD unto these bones; Behold, I will cause breath to enter into you, and ye shall live:
- → (1 Cor 15:45) ... And so it is written, The first man Adam was made a living soul; the last Adam was made a quickening spirit.

(2:9) ... Adam and Eve's sin separated them from the tree of life thus, kept them from obtaining eternal life. Interestingly, the tree of life again appears in a description in Revelation 22 of people enjoying eternal life with God.

- → (Prov 11:30) ... The fruit of the righteous is a tree of life; and he that winneth souls is wise

Tree of Life

Love, Joy, Peace, Faith, Gentleness, Goodness, Meekness, Temperance, Happiness, Longsuffering, Unity

Spirit of God

GOD

Tree of Knowledge of Good and Evil

Human Reasoning, Envy, Jealousy, Vanity, Disharmony, Competition, Strife, Fornication

Spirit of Satan

SATAN

(2:16,17) ... Why would God place a tree in the garden and them forbid Adam to eat from it? God wanted Adam to obey, but he gave him the freedom to choose. Without choice, Adam would have been, like a prisoner, forced to obey. When faced with the choice, chose to obey God.

- → (Deut 30:15) ... See, I have set before thee this day life and good, and death and evil;
- → (Rom 6:23) ... For the wages of sin is death; but the gift of God is eternal life through Jesus Christ our Lord.

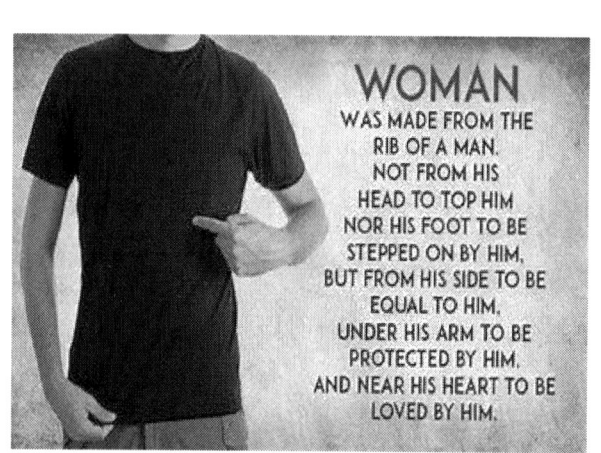

WOMAN WAS MADE FROM THE RIB OF A MAN. NOT FROM HIS HEAD TO TOP HIM NOR HIS FOOT TO BE STEPPED ON BY HIM, BUT FROM HIS SIDE TO BE EQUAL TO HIM, UNDER HIS ARM TO BE PROTECTED BY HIM, AND NEAR HIS HEART TO BE LOVED BY HIM.

(2:28,24) ... He chose, however, to make her from the man's flesh and bone. In doing so, he illustrated for us that in marriage man and woman symbolically become 1 flesh. Throughout the Bible, God treat this special union seriously. The goal in marriage should be more than friendship; it should be oneness.

- → (Prov 18:22) ... Whoso findeth a wife findeth a good thing, and obtaineth favour of the LORD.
- → (1 Cor 11:8—9) ... For the man is not of the woman; but the woman of the man. Neither was the man created for the woman; but the woman for the man.

(2:25) <u>They were not ashamed</u>, but ... After Adam and Eve sinned, embarrassment, shame, and awkwardness followed, creating barriers between themselves and God. We often experience these same barriers in marriage. Like Adam and Eve (3:7), we put on fig leaves (barriers) because we have areas, we don't want our spouse, or God, to know about. Then we hide like Adam and Eve did. In marriage, lack of spiritual, emotional, and intellectual intimacy usually proceeds a breakdown of physical intimacy. In the same way, we fail to expose our secret thoughts to God, we shut down our lines of communication with him.

Satan and his fallen angels were cast out of heaven.

(3:1) ... Satan at one time was an angelic being who rebelled against God and was thrown out of Heaven. As a created being, Satan has definite limitations. Although he is trying to tempt everyone away from God, he will not be the final victor. In (3:14,15), God promises that Satan will be crushed, by the Messiah, Jesus Christ.

- → (2 Cor 11:3) ... But I fear, lest by any means, as the serpent beguiled Eve through his subtilty, so your minds should be corrupted from the simplicity that is in Christ.
- → (Rev 12:9) ... And the great dragon was cast out, that old serpent, called the Devil, and Satan, which deceiveth the whole world: he was cast out into the earth, and his angels were cast out with him.

(3:1—6) ... We must realize that being tempted is not a sin. We have not sinned until we give in to the sin.

To resist temptation, we must:

1. Pray for strength to resist.
2. Run, sometimes literally.
3. Say no when confronted with what we know is wrong.
    → (James 1:12) ... Blessed is the man that endureth temptation: for when he is tried, he shall receive the crown of life, which the Lord hath promised to them that love him.

- Satan tempted Eve by getting her to doubt God's goodness. He suggested that God was strict, stingy, and selfish for not wanting Eve to share his knowledge of good and evil. Satan made Eve forget all God had given her and focus on the one thing she couldn't have. We fall into trouble when we focus on the few things we don't have, rather on the countless things God has given us. The next time that you are feeling sorry for yourself of what you don't have, consider all the things you do have and thank God, then your doubts wont led you to sin.

(3:5) ... We sometimes have the illusion that freedom is doing anything we want. God say true freedom comes from obedience and knowing what not to do. The restrictions he gives us are for our good, showing us how to avoid evil. Don't listen to Satan's temptations.

To become more like is humanity's highest goal. It is what we are suppose to do. But Satan misled Eve on the right way to accomplish this goal. He told her, that she could be more like God by defying God's authority; by taking God's place and deciding for herself what was best for her life. In effect, he told her to become her own god.

But to become like God is to reflect his characteristics and recognize his authority over your life. Self-exaltation leads to rebellion against God. As soon as we begin to leave God out of our plans, we are placing ourselves above him. This is exactly what Satan wants us to do.

(3:6) ... Our sins do not always appear ugly to us, and the pleasant sins are the hardest to avoid. So, prepare yourself for the attractive temptations, that come your way. We cannot always prevent temptation but there is always a way of escape (1 Cor 10:13).

When we do something wrong, often we try to relieve our guilt by involving someone else. Like poison spilled in a river, sin swiftly spreads. Recognize and confess your sin to God before you are tempted to pollute those around you.

- → (Jam 1:14—15) ... But every man is tempted, when he is drawn away of his own lust, and enticed. Then when lust hath conceived, it bringeth forth sin: and sin, when it is finished, bringeth forth death.
- → (1 John 2:16) ... For all that is in the world, the lust of the flesh, and the lust of the eyes, and the pride of life, is not of the Father, but is of the world.

(3:7) … A guilty conscious is a warning signal God places inside of you that goes off when you have done wrong. The worst thing you could do is eliminate the guilty feeling without eliminating the cause. Be glad those guilty feelings are there. They make you aware of your sin, so you can ask God for forgiveness, and then you can correct your wrongdoing.

(3:8) … God wanted to be with them, but because of their sin, they where afraid to show themselves. Sin had broken their fellowship with God, just as it has broken ours. But through Jesus, the way has been open for us to renew our fellowship with him. God longs to be with us. He actively offers us his unconditional love. Our natural response is fear, for we know that we can't live up to his standards on our own. But recognizing that he loves us, regardless of our faults, can help remove dread.

→ (Job 31:33) … If I covered my transgressions as Adam, by hiding mine iniquity in my bosom:

SATAN'S PLAN

DOUBT ➔ QUESTION GOD

DISCOURAGE ➔ LOOK AT OUR PROBLEMS NOT GOD

DIVERSION ➔ MAKES WRONG LOOK GOOD

DEFEAT ➔ FEEL LIKE A FAILURE AND GIVE UP

DELAY ➔ PUT OFF DOING THINGS

(3:14) ... Adam and Eve chose their course of action "disobedience", and then God chose his. As a holy God, he could only respond in a way consistent with his perfect moral nature. He couldn't allow sin to go unchecked; he had to punish it. We sin today because of the sin of Adam and Eve, that was set in motion. Everyone born, other than Jesus, had inherited the sinful nature of Adam and Eve (Rom 5:12—21). Adam and Eve's punishment reflects how serious God's view of any kind of sin.

> → (Deut 28:15) ... But it shall come to pass, if thou wilt not hearken unto the voice of the LORD thy God, to observe to do all his commandments and his statutes which I command thee this day; that all these curses shall come upon thee, and overtake thee:

(3:15) ... Satan is our enemy. He will do anything he can to get us to follow his evil, deadly plan. "Thou shalt bruise his heel" refers to Satan's repeated attempts to defeat Christ. "It shall bruise thy head" foreshadows Satan's defeat when Christ rose from the dead. A bruise on a heel isn't deadly but a strike on the head is. Already God was revealing his plan to defeat Satan and offer salvation through Jesus.

> → (Rom 16:20) ... And the God of peace shall bruise Satan under your feet shortly. The grace of our Lord Jesus Christ be with you. Amen.

(3:22-24) ... Life in the Garden of Eden was like living in Heaven. Everything was perfect, and if Adam and Eve had obeyed God, they could have lived there forever. But after disobeying, Adam and Eve no longer deserved Paradise, and God told them to leave. Like Adam and Eve, all of us have sinned and are separated from fellowship with God. We don't have to stay separated, however. God will be preparing a new earth as an eternal paradise for his people (Rev 21—22).

To build a relationship with God, We must:

1. Drop our excuses and self-defense.
2. Stop trying to hide from God.
3. We must become convinced that God's way is better than our way.

GENESIS
Cain & Abel

(4:1) ... The word "Knew" means "had sexual intercourse with" sexual union = oneness and total knowledge of another person. Sexual intercourse is the most intimate of acts, sealing a social, physical, and spiritual relationship. This is why God has it reserved for marriage alone.

(4:2) ... Adam and Eve, now had to struggle against the elements in order to provide food, clothing, and shelter for themselves and their family. Cain became a farmer, while Abel was a shepherd

(4:3-5) ... God evaluates both our motives and the quality of what we offer him. We should not worry about how much we are giving up, for all things are God's in the 1st place. Instead, we should joyfully give to God our best in time, money, possessions, and talents.

(Heb 11:4) ... By faith Abel offered unto God a more excellent sacrifice than Cain, by which he obtained witness that he was righteous, God testifying of his gifts: and by it he being dead yet speaketh.

(4:6,7) ... After Cain's Sacrifice was rejected, God gave him the chance to make right his wrongs and try again. God even encouraged him to. But Cain refused and the rest of his life was an example of what happens to those who refuse to admit their mistakes.

(Jonah 4:4) ... Then said the LORD, Doest thou well to be angry?

(James 1:15) ... Then when lust hath conceived, it bringeth forth sin: and sin, when it is finished, bringeth forth death.

(4:8—10) ... Simple disobedience suddenly degenerated into outright murder. Adam and Eve acted only against God, but Cain acted against both God and man. A small sin has a way of growing out of control. Let God help you with your "little" sins before they turn into tragedies.

(1 John 3:12) ... Not as Cain, who was of that wicked one, and slew his brother. And wherefore slew he him? Because his own works were evil, and his brothers righteous.

(Num 35:33) ... So ye shall not pollute the land wherein ye are: for blood it defileth the land: and the land cannot be cleansed of the blood that is shed therein, but by the blood of him that shed it.

(Heb 12:24) ... And to Jesus the mediator of the new covenant, and to the blood of sprinkling, that speaketh better things than that of Abel.

Genesis 3	Genesis 4
The Serpent comes and deceives Eve	God warns Cain that sin is crouching at the door
Adam and Eve eat of the forbidden fruit	Cain murders his brother
Adam and Eve begin the cycle of sin	Cain continues the cycle of sin
God comes in the cool of the day to seek out and question Adam and Eve	God comes to seek out and question Cain about his brother

(4:11-15) ... Cain was severely punished for this murder. God judges all sin and punishes appropriately, but not simply out of anger or vengeance. Rather, God's punishment is meant to correct us and restore our fellowship with him. When you are corrected, don't resent it, but renew your fellowship with God.

We have only heard of 4 people so far: Adam, Eve, Cain, and Abel. Where did he get his wife (4:17)? Adam and Eve had numerous children: they had been told to "replenish the earth" (1:28). The wife Cain chose may have been a sister or a niece. The human race was still genetically pure and there was no fear of side effects for marring relatives.

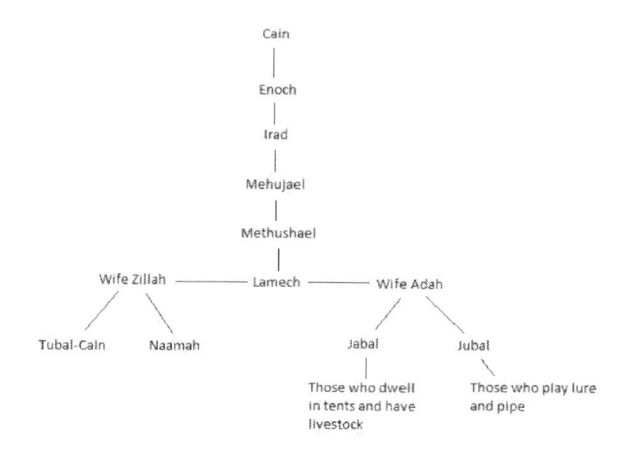

```
                    Cain
                     |
                    Enoch
                     |
                    Irad
                     |
                   Mehujael
                     |
                  Methushael
                     |
Wife Zillah ——— Lamech ——— Wife Adah
   /    \            /      \
Tubal-Cain Naamah  Jabal    Jubal
                     |         \
              Those who dwell   Those who play lure
              in tents and have and pipe
              livestock
```

(4:18—26) … This short summary of Lamech's family shows us the variety of talent and ability God gives humans. It also presents the continuous development of sin as times passes. Another murder has occurred, presumably in self-defense.

2 groups are appearing:

1. Those who show indifference to sin and evil.
2. Those who call upon the name of the Lord. (descendants of Seth, 4:26)

Seth would take Abel's place as leader of the line of God's faithful people.

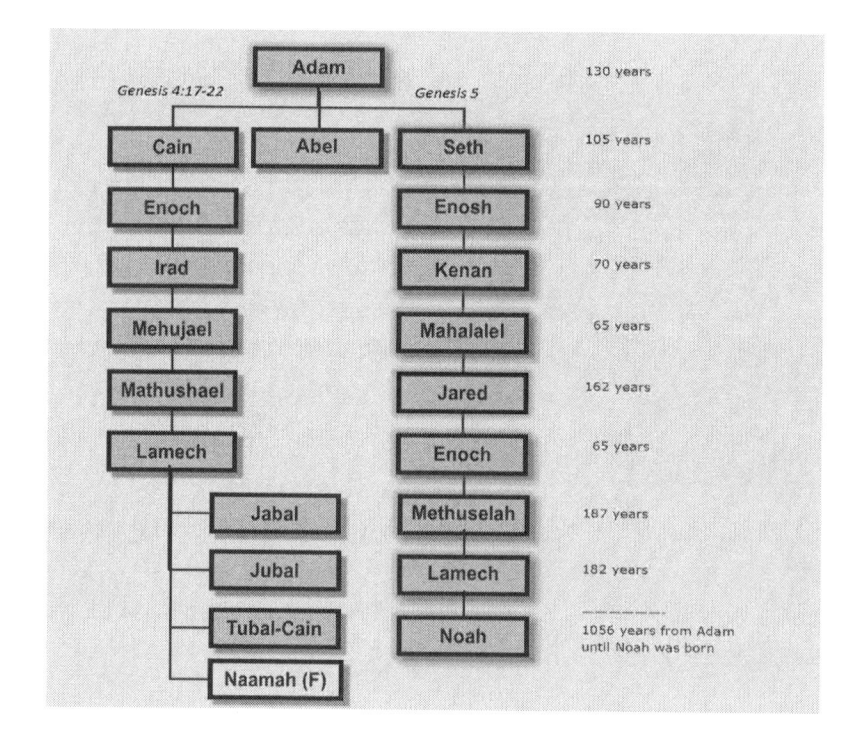

Genesis 4:17-22	Adam	Genesis 5	
			130 years
Cain	Abel	Seth	105 years
Enoch		Enosh	90 years
Irad		Kenan	70 years
Mehujael		Mahalalel	65 years
Mathushael		Jared	162 years
Lamech		Enoch	65 years
Jabal		Methuselah	187 years
Jubal		Lamech	182 years
Tubal-Cain		Noah	1056 years from Adam until Noah was born
Naamah (F)			

```
                              Adam 930
        ┌──────────┬──────────┼──────────────────┐
       Cain       Abel       Seth 912      Other Sons & Daughters
        │                     │
       Enoch                 Enos 905
        │                     │
       Irad                  Cainan 910
        │                     │
       Mehujael              Mahalaleel 895
        │                     │
       Methusael             Jared 962
        │                     │
       Lamech                Enoch 365
    ┌────┬────┬────┐          │
  Jubal Jabal Naamah Tubal-Cain  Methuselah 969
                               │
                              Lamech 777
                               │
                              Noah 950
                         Ham  Shem 600  Japheth
```

(5:1) ... Genealogies were added to and passed down from family to family. Even more important than preserving family tradition, genealogies were included to confirm Bible promises that the coming Messiah, Jesus Christ, would be born in the line of Abraham.

(5:21—24) ... At 1st it looks as if Enoch fared worse than the other patriarchs: He lived on earth 365 years? Hebrews 11:5 explains what verse 24 means: Enoch was taken directly to heaven without seeing death. Enoch, then, lived longer than any of the other patriarchs, for he never died at all.

(Heb 11:5) ... By faith Enoch was translated that he should not see death; and was not found, because God had translated him: for before his translation he had this testimony, that he pleased God.

How did people live so long?

1. The human race was genetically purer in the early time period, so there were less diseases to shorten the life span.
2. The "waters which were above the firmament" (1:7), kept out harmful cosmic rays and shielded people from environmental factors that haste aging.
3. God gave people longer lives so they would have time to "replenish the earth" (1:28), and make a significant impact for him.

THE STORY OF NOAH (6:1—11:32)

Earth was no longer the perfect paradise that God intended. It is frightening to see how quickly all of humanity forgot about God. Incredibly, in all the world, only one man and his family still worshipped God. That man was Noah. Because of his faithfulness and obedience, God saved him and his whole family from a vast flood that destroyed every other human being on earth. This section shows us how God hates sin and judges those who enjoy it.

Noah was spared from the destruction of the flood because he obeyed God and built a boat. Just as God protected Noah and his family, he still protects those who are faithful to him today.

NOAH

The story of Noah's life involves not one, but 2 great and tragic floods. The world in Noah's day was flooded with evil, of God's people, only Noah remembered the God of creation, perfection, and love. God's response to the severe situation was a 120 year long last chance, during which he had Noah build a graphic illustration of the message of his life. For Noah, obedience meant a long-term commitment to a project. Many of us have problems sticking to any project, whether or not, it is directed by God. It is interesting that the length of Noah's obedience is longer than the life-span of people today. Our only comparable long-term project is our very lives. Perhaps this is one great challenge Noah's life gives us—to live an entire lifetime of obedience and gratitude.

Noah's Strengths and Accomplishments

- The only follower left in his generation. 2nd father of the human race.
- Man of patience, consistency, and obedience.
- 1st major shipbuilder.

Noah's Weaknesses and Mistakes

- He got drunk and embarrassed himself in front of his sons.

Lessons from Noah's Life

- God is faithful to those who obey him
- God doesn't always protect us from trouble, but loves us spite trouble.
- Obedience is a life-long commitment
- A man maybe faithful, but his sinful nature travels with him.

Vital Statistics

- WHERE: not sure how far from the Garden of Eden that the people settled.
- OCCUPATION: farmer, shipbuilder, and preacher.
- RELATIVES: Grandfather ➔ Methuselah
  - Father ➔ Lamech
  - Sons ➔ Ham, Shem, Japheth, others not mentioned.

(6:3) … What patience God showed, allowing the people of Noah's day 120 years to change their sinful ways. God shows his great patience with us as well. While 120 years seems long, eventually the time ran out and the flood waters swept across the earth. Your time also may be running out. Turn to God to forgive your sins.

    (1 Peter 3:20) … Which sometime were disobedient, when once the longsuffering of God waited in the days of Noah, while the ark was a preparing, wherein few, that is, eight souls were saved by water.

(6:4) … The giants mentioned here, most likely, used their physical advantage to oppress the people around them.

    (Num 13:33) … And there we saw the giants, the sons of Anak, which come of the giants: and we were in our own sight as grasshoppers, and so we were in their sight.

(6:7) … Did God regret create humanity? No, God does not change his mind (1 Sam 15:29). He was expressing sorrow for what the people had done to themselves, as a parent does towards our rebellious child. God was sorry they chose sin and death instead of a relationship with him.

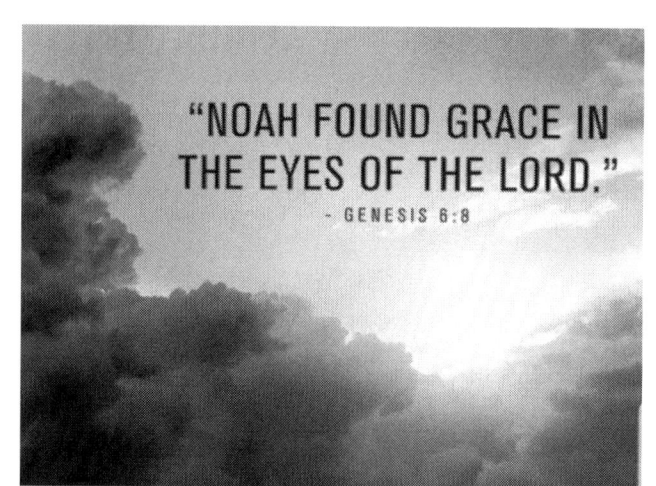

"NOAH FOUND GRACE IN THE EYES OF THE LORD."
- GENESIS 6:8

(6:8) … Our sin breaks God's heart as much as sin did in Noah's day. We can follow Noah's example and find "grace in the eyes of the Lord" in spite of the sin that surrounds us.

(6:9) ... To say that Noah was "perfect in his generation" does not mean that he never sinned, it means that he wholeheartedly loved and obeyed God. Like Noah, we live in a world filled with evil. Are we influencing others or are we being influenced by them?

    (Eze 14:14) ... Though these three men, Noah, Daniel, and Job, were in it, they should deliver but their own souls by their righteousness, saith the Lord GOD.

(6:22) ... Today things haven't changed much. Each day 1000's of people are warned of God's inevitable judgement, yet most of them don't believe it will happen.

(7:16) ... Many have wondered how this animal kingdom round-up happened. God took care of the details of that job while Noah was doing his part by building the ark. Like Noah, concentrate on the things God has given you to do, and leave the rest to him.

(7:17—24) ... Remember, God's reason for sending the flood was to destroy all the earth's wickedness. It would have taken a major flood to accomplish this.

(Job 12:15) ... Behold, he withholdeth the waters, and they dry up: also, he sendeth them out, and they overturn the earth.

(8:6—16) ... Noah occasionally sent out a bird to test the earth and see if it was dry, but he didn't go out until God told him to. He was waiting for God's timing. We like Noah, must trust God to give us patience during these difficult times, when we must wait.

(8:22) ... God has promised never again to destroy everything on earth until the judgement day, when Jesus returns to destroy evil, forever. Now every change of season is a reminder of his promise.

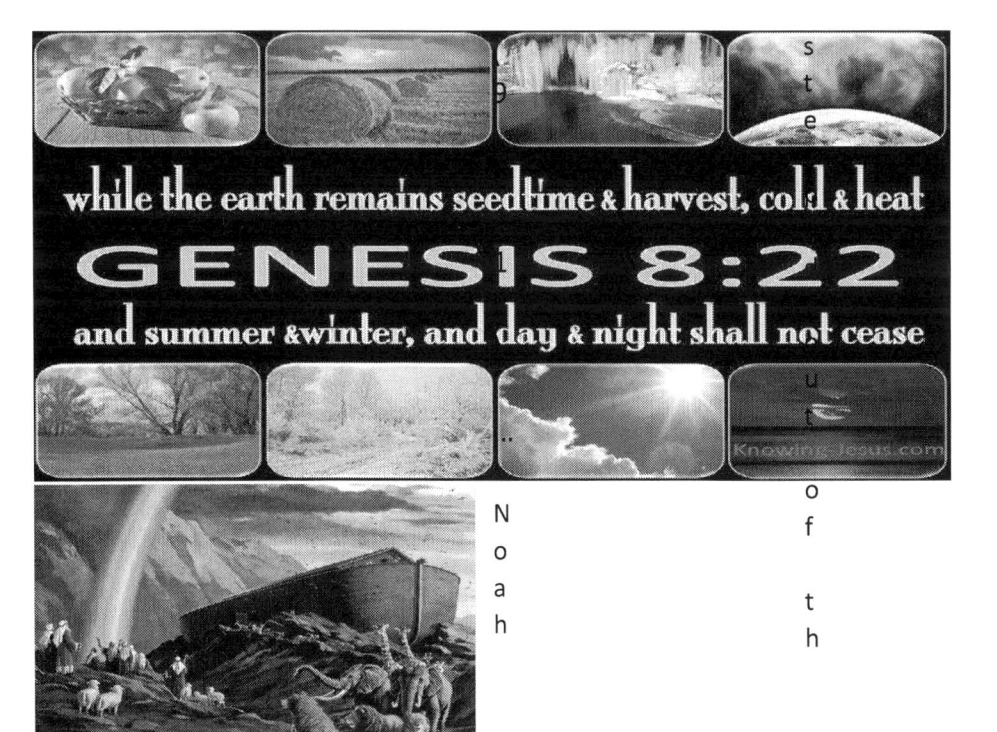

while the earth remains seedtime & harvest, cold & heat
GENESIS 8:22
and summer & winter, and day & night shall not cease

Noah

of
th

stepped

out
of
the

ark
onto
earth

1. Never again will a flood do such destruction.
2. As the world remains, seasons will come as expected.
3. The rainbow will be a sign, that God keeps his promises. This is still true today.

human life

(9:20—27) ... Noah, the great hero of faith, got drunk—a poor example of godliness to his sons. This story shows us that even goldy people sin and their bad influence effects their families. Ham's mocking attitude revealed a severe lack of respect for his father and for God.

(Hab 2:15) ... Woe unto him that giveth his neighbour drink, that puttest thy bottle to him, and makest him drunken also, that thou mayest look on their nakedness!

Noah's curse was at the Canaanite nation—a nation God knew would become wicked. The curse was fulfilled when the Israelites entered the Promised Land and drove the Canaanites out (Joshua).

JAPHETH
Greeks Thracians Scythians

God gave him a reassuring promise, or covenant, which had 3 parts:

Bible Nations Descended from Noah's Sons

NOAH

Canaanites
Egyptians Philistines
Hittites Amorites

1:13 1

Hebrews

Chaldeans

Assyrians

Persians

Syrians

Where the Descendants Settled

For the most part, **JAPHETH'S** descendants settled

- Europe
- Asia Minor

HAM'S descendants settled in
- Canaan
- Egypt
- Africa

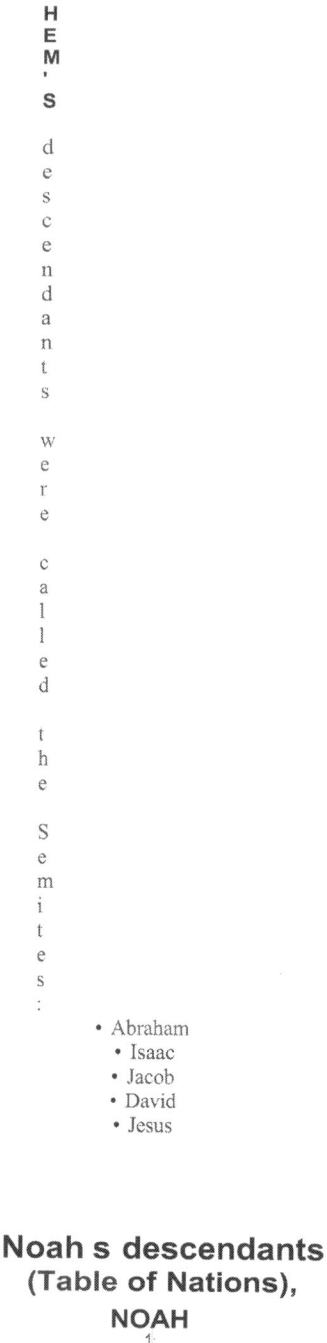

SHEM'S descendants were called the Semites:
- Abraham
- Isaac
- Jacob
- David
- Jesus

Noah's descendants
(Table of Nations),
NOAH

Japheth	Shem	Ham
Gomer, M'agiog Madai, Javan, TU1bal Me.shech. Tir,as	E.lam, Asshu r. Ar.phaxad, lud, Aram	Cush, MIzralm Phut, Canaa.n
Sons of Gomer Ashkenaz Togarmah	Son of Arphaxad Sail-ah :Ripha-th,	Sons of Cush Seba H.a:vilaih, Saibt.af.'l

Sons of Javan
Elishah, Tarshish
Kittim, Dodanim

Son of Salah
Eber

Sons of Eber
Peleg, Joktan

Sons of Joktan
Almodad, Shaleph
Hazarmaveth, Jerah
Hadoram, Uzal, Diklah
Obal, Abimael, Sheba
Ophir, Havilah, Jobab

Sons of Aram
Uz, Hul, Gether, Mash

Raamah, Sabtecha, Nimrod

Sons of Raamah
Sheba, Dedan

Sons of Mizraim
Ludim, Anamim
Lehabim, Naphtuhim
Pathrusim, Casluhim
Caphtorim

Sons of Canaan
Sidon, Heth, Jebusite
Amorite, Girgashite, Hivite
Arkite, Sinite, Arvadite
Zemarite, Hamathite

biblestudy.org

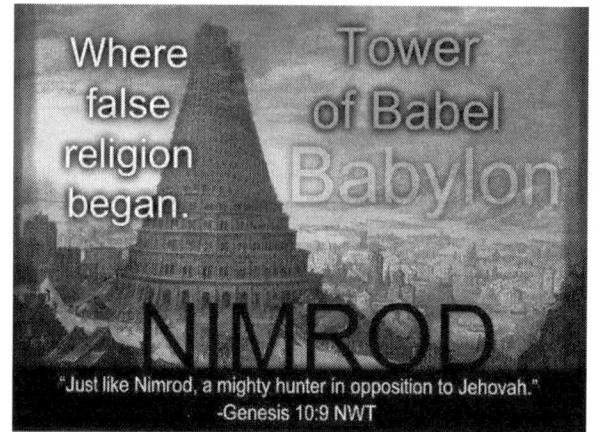

(10:8—10) ... Not much is known about Nimrod except he was a mighty hunter. People with great gifts can become proud, which is probably what happened to him.

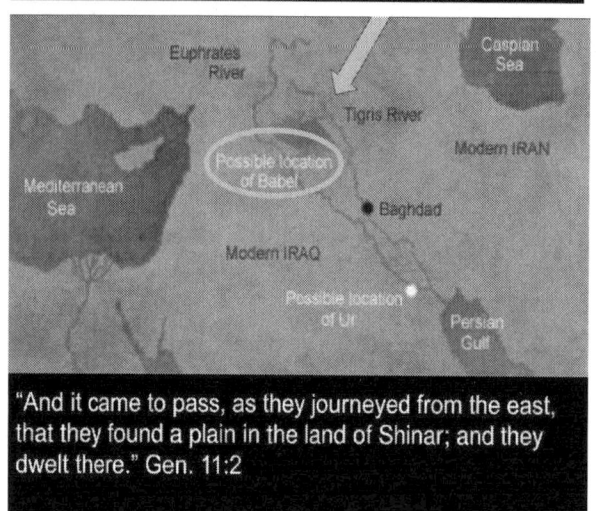

(11:1-4) ... The plain between the Tigris and Euphrates Rivers offered a perfect location for the city and tower, "who's top may reach unto Heaven."

The tower of Babel was most likely a ziggurat, used commonly at this time. Often built like temples, they looked like pyramids with steps or ramps leading up the sides. They stood as high as 300 ft and were often just as wide; they were the focal point on the city. The people here built their tower as a monument to their own greatness. It was a great monument for themselves rather than to God. When we build things to draw attention to our achievements, when used to give us identity and self-worth, they have God's place in our lives.

Are there "towers" like this in your life?

The Tower of Babel

The Tower of Babel would have been built in ziggurat form. It probably was ancient Babylon's Etemenanki—the "temple of the foundation of heaven and earth." Many Babylonian legends and documents describe this structure, as does the Greek historian Herodotus.

Ancients believed that deities dwelt on high places and associated the gods with hills and mountains. Babylon was on low ground—the ziggurat was a substitute mountain. It towered above the dust in the lower air and was an excellent place to observe the stars. From a ziggurat's top, heaven seemed closer.

Levels shown: Level 1, Level 2, Level 3, Level 4, Level 5, Level 6, Level 7 (with Stairs)

The Egagila Tablet from Uruk describes the Etemenanki with these dimensions. The stairs for the top levels are interior.

Size comparison (approximate)

Great Pyramid of Giza (tallest building in the ancient world)
Height 430', base 755.5'

Tower of Babel
Height 300', base 300'

Monadnock Building in Chicago (tallest brick-structure building now standing)
Height 197', base 62' (16 floors)

Tower of Babel (t<>pv)

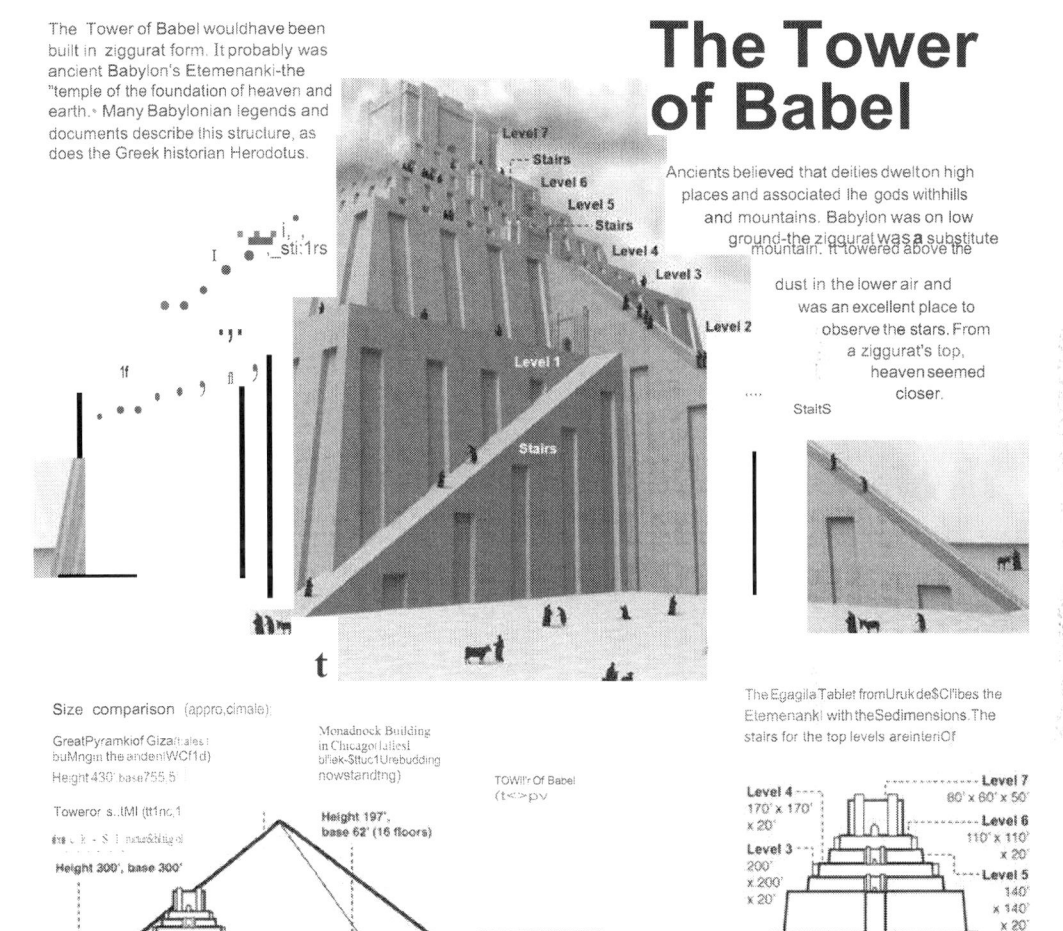

American Football field

Level 4 — 170' x 170' x 20'
Level 3 — 200' x 200' x 20'
Level 6 — 110' x 110' x 20'
Level 5 — 140' x 140' x 20'
Level 7 — 80' x 60' x 50'

GRAPHIC BY KARBEIMULTIMEDIA. COPYRIGHT 2011 LOGOS BIBLE SOFTWARE

The Genealogy of Shem

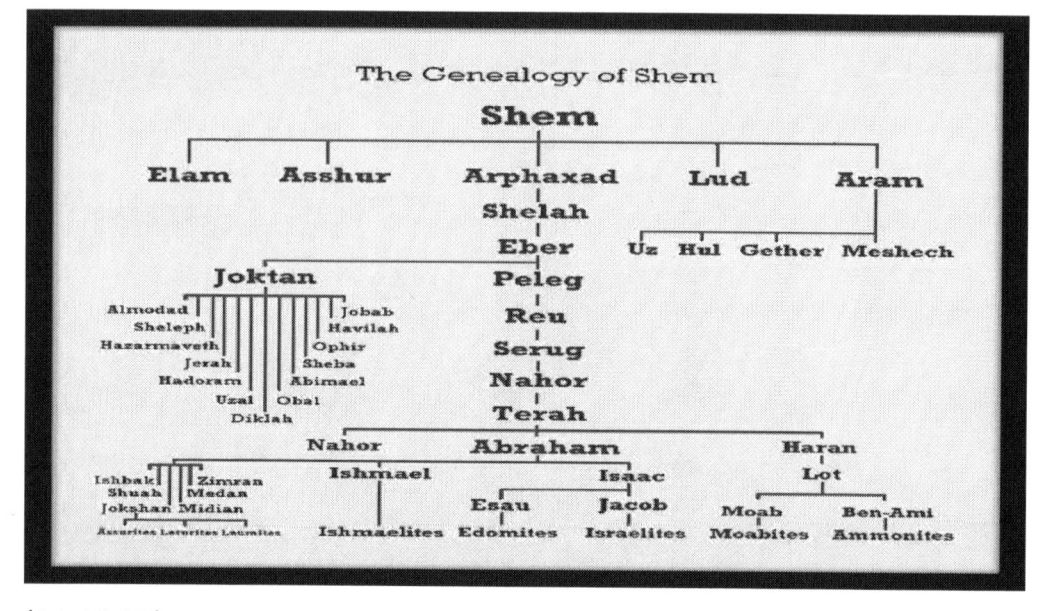

Shem
- Elam
- Asshur
- Arphaxad
  - Shelah
    - Eber
      - Joktan
        - Almodad, Sheleph, Hazarmaveth, Jerah, Hadoram, Uzal, Diklah, Obal, Abimael, Sheba, Ophir, Havilah, Jobab
      - Peleg
        - Reu
          - Serug
            - Nahor
              - Terah
                - Nahor
                  - Ishbak, Shuah, Jokshan, Zimran, Medan, Midian
                    - Asshurites, Letushites, Leummites
                  - Ishmael
                    - Ishmaelites
                - Abraham
                  - Isaac
                    - Esau → Edomites
                    - Jacob → Israelites
                - Haran
                  - Lot
                    - Moab → Moabites
                    - Ben-Ami → Ammonites
- Lud
- Aram
  - Uz, Hul, Gether, Meshech

(11:10-27) ... We have a list of Shem's descendants, who are blessed (9:26). From Shem's line comes Abram and the entire Jewish nation, which would eventually conquer the land of Canaan in the days of Joshua.

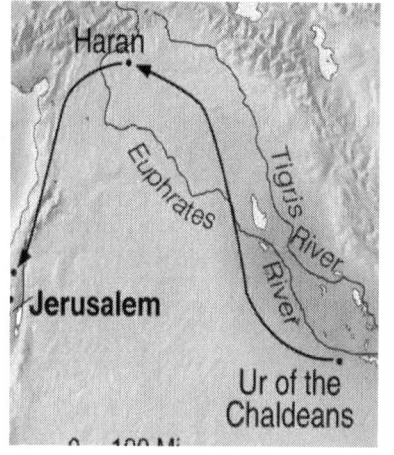

Abraham grew up in Ur of the Chaldeans, an important city in the ancient world. The city carried on an extensive trade with its neighbors and has a vast library. Growing up in Ur, Abraham was most likely well educated.

Terah, Abram's father, left Ur to go to Canaan; but settled in Haran instead. Why did he stop ½ way? Could have been fear, health, or even climate. But this did not change Abram's calling. He had respect for his father's leadership, but when Terah died, Abram moved to Canaan. God's will may come in stages. Just as the time in Haran was a transition period for Abram, so God may give us transition periods and times of waiting to help us depend on him and trust his timing. If we patiently do his will during this transition time, we will be better prepared to serve him as we should when he calls us.

ABRAHAM

Abraham had a choice to make. His decision was between setting out with his family and belongings for parts unknown or staying right where he was. He had to decide between the security he already had and the uncertainty of traveling under God's direction. All he had to go on was God's promise to guide and bless him. Abraham could hardly have been expected to visualize how much of the future was resting on his decision of whether to go or to stay, but his obedience affected the history of the world. His decision to follow God set in motion the development of the nation that God would eventually use as his own, when he visited the earth himself. When Jesus Christ came to the earth, God's promise was fulfilled; through Abraham the entire world was blessed.

You probably don't know the long-term effects of most decisions you make. But shouldn't the fact that there will be long-term results cause you to think more carefully and seek God's guidance as you make choices and take action today?

Abraham's Strength's and Accomplishments

- His faith pleased God and was the founder of the Jewish nation.
- Was respected and courageous in defending his family.
- He was a caring father and practiced hospitality to others.
- Successful and wealthy rancher.

Abraham's Weaknesses and Mistakes

- Under direct pressure, he distorted the truth

Lessons from Abraham's Life

- God desires dependance, trust, and faith in him—not faith in our ability to please him
- God's plan from the beginning has been to male himself known to all people.

Vital Statistics

- WHERE: Born in Ur of the Chaldeans, but mostly lived in Canaan.
- OCCUPATION: Wealthy livestock owner
- RELATIVES: Brothers ➔ Nahor & Haran
    Father ➔ Terah
    Wife ➔ Sarah
    Nephew ➔ Lot
    Sons ➔ Ishmale & Isaac
- CONTEMORARIES: Abimelech & Melchizedek

SARAH

There probably isn't much things harder than wait. One way we often cope with a short or long-term wait is to begin helping God get his plan in action. Sarah tried this approach. She was too old to expect to have a child of her own, so she thought God must have something else in mind. For Sarah's limited point of view this could only be to give Abraham a son through another woman—a common practice in her day. The plan seemed harmless enough. Sarah would take the child as her own. The plan worked beautifully—at 1st. Throughout the story, Sarah regretted the day she decided to push God's timetable ahead.

Another way we cope with a long wait is to gradually conclude that what we're waiting for in never going to happen. Sarah waited 90 years for a baby! When God told her that she will finally have one of her own, she laughed, not so much from a lack of faith in what God could do, but from doubt in what he could do through her. When confronted about her laughter, she lied—as she had seen her husband do from time to time. She probably didn't want her true feelings known.

What part of your life seem to be "on hold" right now? Do you understand that this may be part of God's plan for you? The Bible has more than enough clear direction to keep us busy while were waiting for some particular part of life to move ahead.

Sarah's Strengths and Accomplishments

- She was loyal to her own child. She became a mother of a nation and ancestor of Jesus.
- She was a Woman of Faith. She was the 1st woman listed in the Hall of Faith in Hebrews 11.

Sarah's Weaknesses and Mistakes

- Had trouble believing God's promises to her.
- Worked out problems without consulting God.
- Tried to cover her faults by blaming others.

Lessons from Sarah's Life

- God responds to faith even in the midst of failure.
- God is not bound to what usually happens; he can stretch the limits and cause unheard-of events to occur.

Vital Statistics

- WHERE: Married Abraham in Ur of the Chaldeans then moved with him to Canaan.
- OCCUPATION: Wife, mother, and household manager.
- RELATIVES: Father-in-law ➔ Terah
    Husband ➔ Abraham
    Son ➔ Isaac

LOT

While still young, Lot lost his father. He had 2 good role models: his grandfather Terah and his uncle Abraham, who raised him. All through his life he was caught up in the present moment, not thinking of the consequences of his actions. By the time that Lot drifted out of the picture, his life had taken an ugly turn. He so blended into the sinful culture, that he didn't want to leave. Then his daughter's committed inset with him. His drifting took him to destruction. Even though Moab was born as a result of Lot's incestuous relationship with one of his daughters; Ruth, great-grandmother of David, ancestor of Jesus, was from Moab. Lot's story gives us hope to us that God forgives and often brings out positive circumstances from evil.

If you are a drifter, the choice for God may seem different, but it is the one choice that puts all other choices in a different light.

Lot's Strengths and Accomplishments

- He was a successful businessman

Lot's Weaknesses and Mistakes

- When faced with decisions, he chose the easiest course of action.
- When given a choice, his 1st response was thinking of himself.

Lessons from Lot's Life

- God wants us to so more than just drift through life; he wants us to be an influence for him.

Vital Statistics

- WHERE: Lived 1st in Ur of the Chaldeans, then moves to Canaan, eventually moved to Sodom.
- OCCUPATION: Wealthy sheep and cattle rancher and a city official.
- RELATIVES: Father ➔ Haran …… Adopted by ➔ Abraham
  Wife & daughters➔ unknown names

½ son & ½ grandsons➔ Moab (Moabites) and Ben-ammi (children of Ammon)

THE STORY OF ABRAHAM … (12:1—25:18)

God appeared to Abraham one day and promised to make his descendants into a great nation. Abraham's part of the agreement was to obey God. Throughout sharp testing and an incident that almost destroyed his family, Abraham remained faithful to God. In this section we will discover how to live a life of faith.

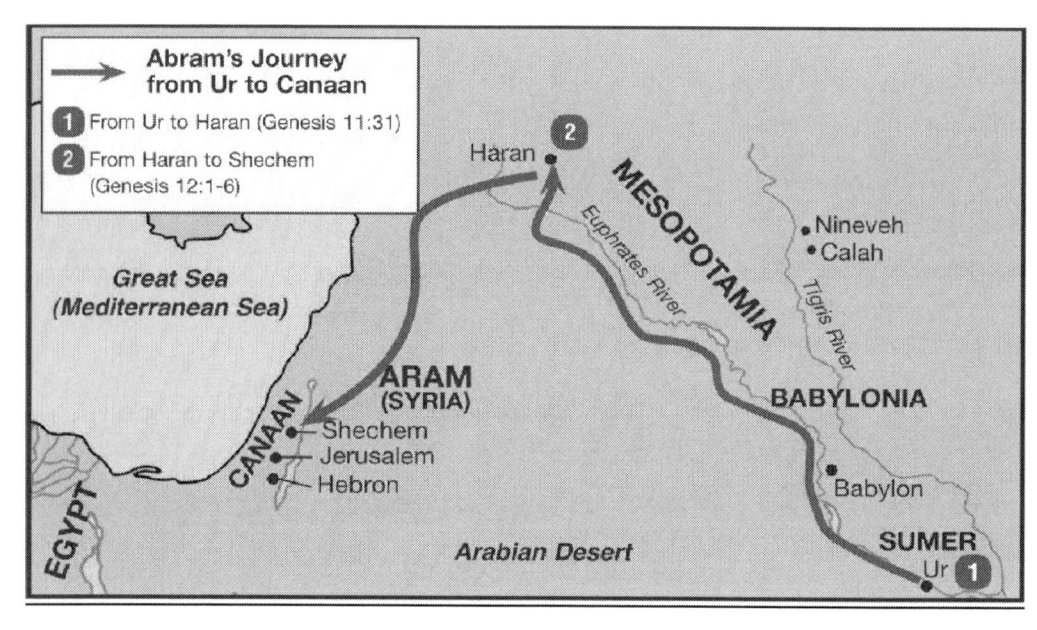

Abram, Sarai, and Lot traveled from Ur of the Chaldeans to Canaan by way of Haran. Through indirect, this route followed the rivers rather than attempting to cross the vast desert.

(Acts 7:3) … And said unto him, get thee out of thy country, and from thy kindred, and come into the land which I shall shew thee.

(Heb 11:8) … By faith Abraham, when he was called to go out into a place which he should after receive for an inheritance, obeyed; and he went out, not knowing whither he went.

(12:2) ... God promised to bless Abram and make him great, but there was one condition, Abram had to do what God wanted him to do. This meant leaving his home, friends, and traveling to a land where God promised to build a great nation from Abram's family. Abram obeyed, by walked away from his home, for God's promise of greater things in the future. God may be trying to lead you to a place greater service and usefulness for him. Don't let the comfort and security of your present position make you miss out on God's plan for you.

(12:5) ... God planned to develop a nation of people that we would call his own. He called Abram from the godless, man-centered city of Ur to a fertile region called Canaan, where a God-centered, moral nation could be established. Though small in dimension, the land of Canaan was the focal point for most of the history of Israel, as far as the rise of Christianity. This small land given to one man, Abram, has a tremendous impact of world history.

(12:6) ...

(Deut 11:30) ... Are they not on the other side Jordan, by the way where the sun goeth down, in the land of the Canaanites, which dwell in the champaign over against Gilgal, beside the plains of Moreh?

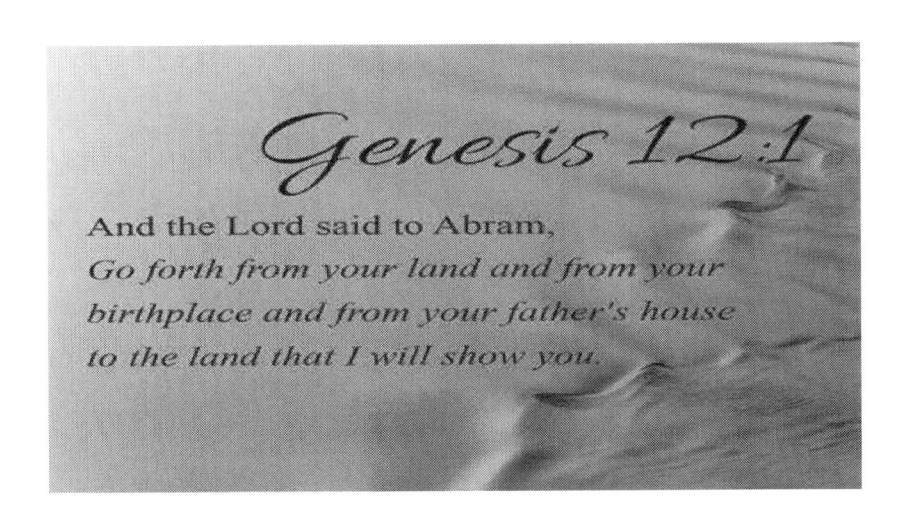

Genesis 12:1

And the Lord said to Abram, Go forth from your land and from your birthplace and from your father's house to the land that I will show you.

ALTARS

(12:7) ... Alters were used in many religions, but for God's people, alters were more than a place of sacrifice. For them, alters symbolized communion with God and commemorated notable encounters with him. Built of rough stones and earth, they often remained in places for years as a continual reminder of God's protection and promises.

2 reasons Abram regularly built alters to God:

- For Prayer and Worship
- To remember God's promise to bless him.

He Couldn't survive spiritually without regularly renewing his love and loyalty to God. Building alters helped Abram remember that God was al the center of his life. Regular worship helps us to remember what God desires and motivates us to obey him.

(Gal 3:16) ... Now to Abraham and his seed were the promises made. He saith not, And to seeds, as of many; but as of one, And to thy seed, which is Christ.

> They left their own land against God's command.
> To Egypt they were bound, where food could be found.

Mediterranean Sea

Egypt **Negev Desert**

(12:10) ... When famine struck, Abram went to Egypt where there was food. A famine in the land, God called him, was a test of faith for Abram. He did not question God, when faced with this difficulty. Many believers find that when they determine to follow God, they immediately encounter great obstacles. The next time you face such test, don't 2nd guess what God is doing.

- A famine could cause the loss of a shepherd's wealth. So Abram traveled through Negev Desert to Egypt, where there was a plenty of food and good land for his flocks.

(12:11—13) ... Abram acting out of fear, asked Sarai to tell a ½ truth by saying she was his sister. She was his ½ sister, as well as, his wife. Abram wanted to deceive the Egyptians, so they didn't kill him to get to Sarai. As a brother, Abram would be given a place of honor. As her husband, he would be killed, as is the only way for Sarai to enter Pharaoh's harem. Abram lost faith in God's protection. This is a lesson in how lying compounds the effect of sin. When he lied, Abram's problems multiplied.

(13:1—2) ... Abram's wealth included money and livestock. These animals were valuable commodity used for food, clothing, tent materials, and sacrifices. They were often traded for goods and services.

(13:5—9) ... Facing a potential conflict with Lot, his nephew, Abram took the initiative in settling the dispute. Abram showed willingness to risk being cheated.

Abram's example shows us:

1. How to respond to difficult family situations.
- Take initiative to resolve conflicts
- Let others have 1st choice, even if you don't get what you want.
- Put family peace above personal desires.

---Surrounded by hostile neighbors, the herdsmen should have pulled together, instead of jealousy tearing them apart. Many Christians argue, while Satan is at work all around them.

2. Rivalries, arguments, and disagreements can be destructive.
- They damage good will, trust, and peace.
- They hamper progress towards important goals.
- They make us self-centered rather than love-centered.

---Jesus, in his final prayer, asked God for his followers to be "one" (John 17:21).

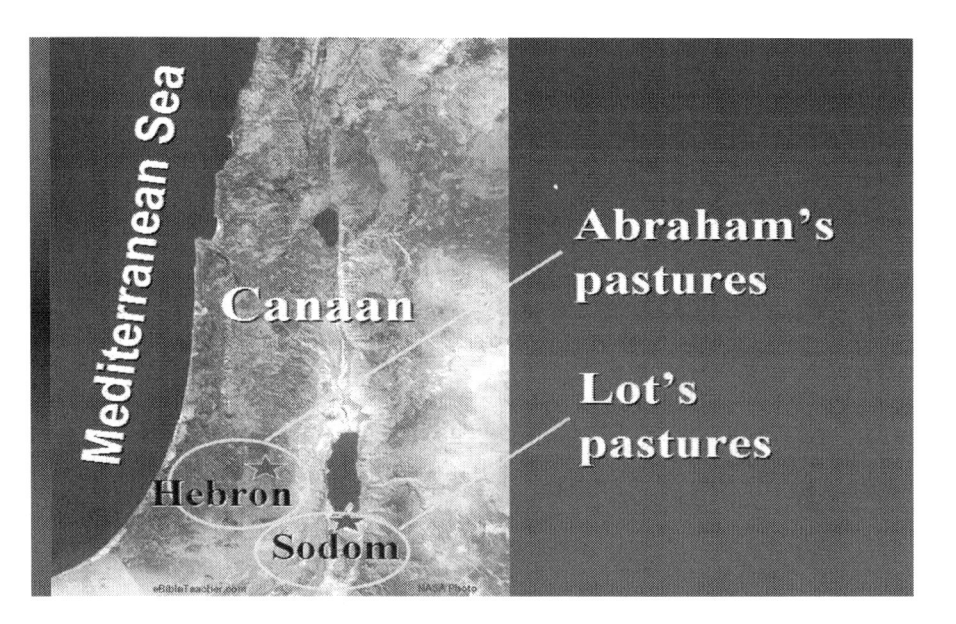

(13:10,11) ... Lot's character is revealed by his choices. He took the best share of land, even if he had to live neat Sodom, city known for sin. He was greedy, not thinking of Abram's needs. We too can choose the best without thinking of other's needs. But like we see with Lot, leads to problems. When we stop making choices in God's direction, we are left with the wrong direction.

(13:12) ... Good pastures and available water seemed like a good choice at 1st. Lot failed to recognize that Sodom's wickedness would lead to temptation, that could destroy his family. Have you chosen to live and work in a Sodom? Even if you are strong enough to resist temptation, other members in your family may not. God commands us to reach people in "Sodom" near us, we must be careful not to become the people we are trying to reach.

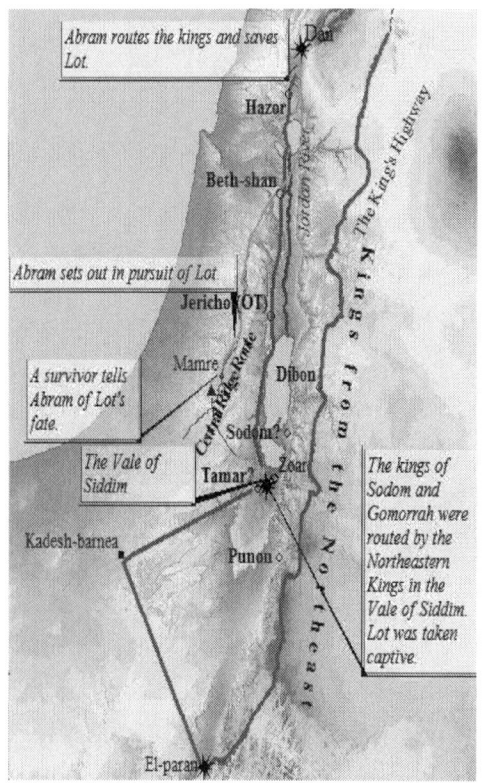

(14:4—16) ... When King Chedorlaomer defeated Sodom, he captured Lot, his family, and his possessions. After conquering Sodom, Chedorlaomer left for his home country, taking many captives with him. Abram learned what had happened, with only 318 men, chased Chedorlaomer's army past Dan and beyond Damascus. There he defeated the king and rescued the captives, among them was Lot and his family. With God's help he won and rescued it all back.

Lot's greedy desires for the best of everything led him into sinful surroundings. This cost him his freedom and enjoyment. As captive, he faced torture, slavery, or death. Prosperity can entice us or enslave us if our motives are not in line with God's desires.

These incidents portray 2 characteristics of Abram:

1) He had courage that came from God.
2) He was prepared by taking time to train his men.
   - Like Abram, we should prepare for difficult takes and take courage from God when they come.
   - Sometimes we must get involved in a messy or painful situation in order to help others.

MELCHIZEDEK

Do you like a mystery? One of the most mysterious people in the Bible is the king of peace, Melchizedek. He appeared one day in the life of Abraham and was not heard of again. What happened that day, however, was to be remembered throughout history and eventually became a subject of the New Testament letter Hebrews. This was a great moment of triumph for Abram. He had just defeated an army and regained freedom for a large group of captives. If there was any doubt in his mind about who's victory it was, Melchizedek set the record straight by reminding Abram, "blessed be the most high God, which hath delivered thy enemies into thy hand" (Gen 14:20). Abram recognized that this man worshipped the same God he did. Do you let God speak to you through other people? In evaluating others, do you consider God's impact on their lives? Are you aware of the similarities between yourself and others who worship God, even if their form of worship is different than yours? Do you know the God of the Bible, well enough, to know if you truly worship him?

Melchizedek's Strengths and Accomplishments

- 1st King/ priest of scripture. Leader with heart tuned to God
- Good at encouraging others to serve God. Character reflected love for God
    — Person in Old Testament who reminds us of Jesus, some believes it was Jesus.

Lessons from Melchizedek's Life

- Lived for God and you will most likely be at the right place—at the right time.

Vital Statistics

- WHERE: Ruled in Salem, site of future Jerusalem.
- OCCUPATION: king of Salem and priest of the most high God.

Story told in (Gen 14:17—20); mentioned in (Ps 110:4); (Heb5—7)

WHO WAS MELCHIZEDEK?

He was obviously a God-fearing man. His name means "King of righteousness" and "King of Peace". (Heb 7:1,2) says he was a "priest of the most high God".

4 main suggested themes:

1) He was a respected king of that region.
2) Name may have been a standing title for all kings in the region.
3) He was a type of Christ, meaning OT teaching close to what Jesus did in a lesson.
4) He was the appearance on earth of the preincarnate Christ in a temp body form.

(Heb 5:6) … As he saith also in another place, Thou art a priest for ever after the order of Melchisedec.

(Heb 7:1) … For this Melchisedec, king of Salem, priest of the most high God, who met Abraham returning from the slaughter of the kings, and blessed him

Genesis 15:1

- Abrahams fears
- Was worried because he had not children of his own
- Genesis 15 likely shortly after Lot was rescued
- Abraham feared retribution from the Mesopotamian kings he had defeated

Why would Abram be afraid? Maybe he feared revenge from the kings he defeated.

God gave him 2 reasons for courage:

- He promised to defend Abram, "I am thy shield".
- He promised to be Abram's "exceeding great reward".

(15:2,3) … Eliezer was Abram's most trusted servant, acting as household administrator "Steward"-in Gen 24. By custom, if Abram was to die without son, his eldest servant would become heir. Although Abram loved his servant, he wanted a son to carry on the family name.

(15:6) … Although human and sinful (mistakes) Abram believed God. It was faith not perfection, that made him right in God's eyes. Same for us: When we believe and put our faith in God, he declares us righteous. Our outward actions will not by themselves make us right with God, but the heartfelt inner confidence that God is who he says he is.

(15:16) … The Amorites were a nation living in Canaan, land God promised Abram. God knew that they would become so wicked that he would give it over to Abram's descendants. God was giving the Amorites plenty of time to repent. God is merciful, knows all, and acts justly—and his timing is perfect.

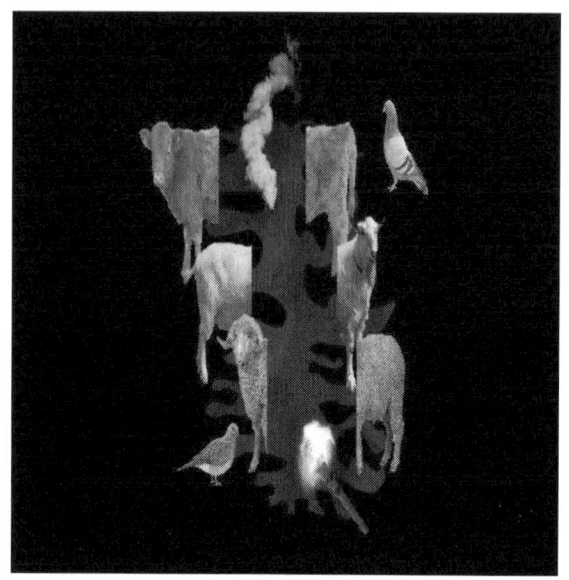

(15:17) ... Why did God send this strange vision to Abram? God's covenant with Abraham was serious business. It represented an incredible promise from God and a huge responsibility for Abram. To confirm his promise, God gave Abram a sign—the smoking furnace and burning lamp. God took the initiative, gave the confirmation, and followed through on his promises. The sign to Abram was a visual assurance to him, that the covenant God had made was real.

HAGAR

Escape of some kind is usually the most tempting solution to our problems. In fact, it can become a habit. Hagar was a person who used that approach. When the going got tough, she usually got going—in the other direction.

However, it is worthwhile to note that the biggest challenges Hagar faced, were brought on by other people's choices. Sarai chose her to bear Abram's child, and Hagar probably had little to say in the matter.

It isn't hard to see how Hagar's pregnancy caused her to look down on Sarai. But that brought on hard feelings, and Sari consequently punished Hagar. This motivated her 1st escape. When she returned to the family and gave birth to Ismael, Sarai's continued barrenness must have contributed to bitterness on both sides.

When Isaac was finally born, Sarai looked for an excuse to have Hagar and Ismael sent away. She found it, when she caught Ishmael teasing Isaac. In the desert, out of water, and facing the death of her son, Hagar once again tried to escape. She walked away so she wouldn't have to watch her son die. Once again, God graciously intervened.

Have you begun to learn that escape is only a temporary solution? God's continual desire is for us to face our problems with his help. Are there problems in your life, in which, you have been using the "Hagar" solution? Choose one of those problems, ask God for help, and begin to face it today.

Hagar's Strengths and Accomplishments

- Mother of Abram's 1st child, Ismael, who became the father of the Arab nation

Hagar's Weaknesses and Mistakes

- When faced with problems, she ran away.
- Pregnancy brought on pride and arrogance.

Lessons from Hagar's Life

- God is faithful to his plans and promises, even when we complicate the process.
- God shows himself as one who knows us and wants to be known by us.

Vital Statistics

- WHERE: Canaan and Egypt
- OCCUPATION: Servant and mother
- RELATIVES: Son → Ishmael

ISHMAEL

His life, his name, and his position were bound up in a conflict between 2 jealous women. His mom, Hagar, servant that she was, agreed to having a child with Abraham; for Sarah. Into this tense atmosphere, Ismael is born. For 13 years, Abram thought that Ishamel being born, fulfilled God's promise. He was surprised, when God said that the promised child, would be his and Sarai's very own. Isaac's birth must have been a devastating impact on Ishmael. He had been treated as a son and heir, but now his future was unclear. As a result, of Ishmael teasing Isaac, him and his mom Hagar, were permanently expelled from the family. Ishmael's life represents the mess we make when we don't try to change the things we could change. To have a changed life, turn to God, trust him to forgive your sinful past, and begin to change your attitude toward him and others.

Ismael's Strengths and Accomplishments

- 1st to experience, sign of covenant to God, Circumcision
- Archer and hunter
- Fathered 12 sons, who became leaders of warrior tribes.

Ishmael's Weaknesses and Mistakes

- Failed to recognize place of his ½ brother, Isaac, and mocked him.

Lessons from Ismael's Life

- God's plans incorporate people's mistakes.

Vital Statistics

- WHERE: Canaan and Egypt
- OCCUPATION: Hunter, archer, and warrior.
- RELATIVES: Parents → Hagar and Abraham
    ½ brother → Isaac

Abraham and Hagar
|
Ishmael and Wife

Mahalath	— Nebaioth
Basemath	— Kedar
	— Adbeel
	— Mibsam
	— Mishma
	— Dumah
	— Massa
	— Hadad
	— Tema
	— Jetur
	— Naphish
	— Kedemah

Kedar → father of Qedarites

    Ancestor of Muhammad

Ishmael daughter → Mahalath (or Bashemath)

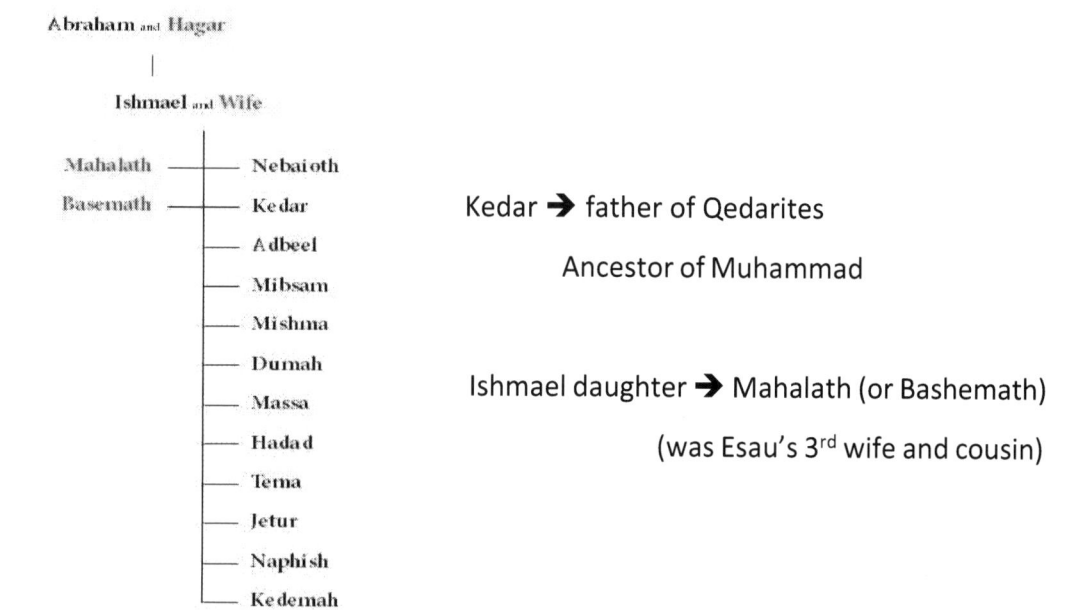

    (was Esau's 3rd wife and cousin)

ISAAC

A name carries great authority. It sets you apart. Many Bible names accomplish even more. They were often descriptions of important facts about one's past and hopes for the future. The choice of the name Isaac, "laughter" for Abraham and Sarah's son must have created a variety of feelings in them each time it was spoken. It must have brought back the joyful feelings of receiving their long-awaited answer to prayer for a child. Most important, it was a testimony to God's power in making his promises a reality.

Isaac was the quiet, "mind my own business" type unless he was specifically called on to take action. HE was the protected only child from the time Sarah got rid of Ishmael until Abraham arranged his marriage to Rebekah. In his own family, Isaac had the patriarchal position, but Rebekah had the power. Rather than stand his ground, Isaac found it easier to compromise or lie to avoid confrontations.

In spite of these shortcomings, Isaac was part of God's plan. Th model his father gave him included a great gift if faith in the one true God. God's promise to create a great nation through which he would bless the world was passed on by Isaac to his twin sons.

It is usually not hard to identify with Isaac, in his weaknesses. But consider, for a moment, that God works through people in spite of their shortcomings and often, through them. As you pray, put into words your desire to be available to God. You will discover that his willingness to use you is even greater than your desire to be used.

Isaac's Strengths and Accomplishments

- Miracle child born to Sarah (90 years old) and Abraham (100 years old)
- Demonstrated great patience.
- 1st descendant to fulfill the promise from God to Abraham.

Isaac's Weaknesses and Mistakes

- Under pressure he tended to lie
- In conflict, he sought to avoid confrontation
- Played favorites between his sons and alienated his wife

Lessons from Isaac's Life

- Patience often brings reward
- God keeps his promises
- Playing favorites is sure to bring family conflicts

Vital Statistics

- WHERE: The area called the Negev, in the southern part of Palestine, between Kadesh and Shur (20:1).
- OCCUPATION: wealthy livestock owner
- RELATIVES: Parents ➔ Abraham and Sarah
    ½ brother ➔
        Ishmael Wife
        ➔ Rebekah
        Sons ➔ Jacob and Esau

Genesis 16

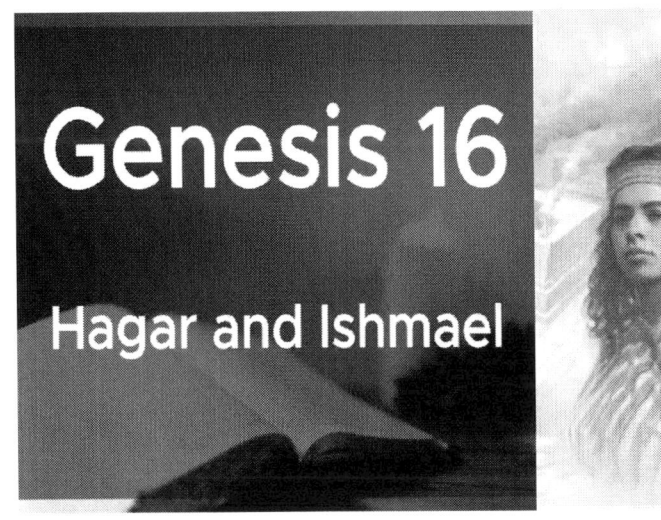

Hagar and Ishmael

(16:1—3) ... Sarai gave Hagar to Abraham as a substitute wife, a common practice at that time. A married woman who could not have children was shamed by her peers and was often required to give a female servant to her husband in order to produce heirs. The children born were considered the children of the wife. Abram was acting within custom, but his actions showed a lack of faith that God would fulfill his promise. Out of this lack of faith came a series of problems. This happens when we take over for God, trying to make a promise of his come true, with efforts not in line with his specific directions.

(16:5) ... Although Sarai arranged for Hagar to have child by Abram, she later blamed Abram, for the results. Its often easier to strike out in frustration and point blame elsewhere, than to admit an error and ask for forgiveness. (Adam and Eve did the same thing in 3:12,13).

(16:6) ... Sarai took out her anger against Abram and herself on Hagar. The treatment was so harsh, Hagar ran away. Anger, raised from our own shortcomings, can be dangerous.

(16:8) ... Hagar was running away from her mistress and her problems.

The anger of the Lord gave her the following advice

- Return and face Sarai (her problem)
- To act as she should

Hagar had to work on her attitude with Sarai, even if it was justified. Running from our problems rarely solves them. We should face our problem, accept God's help, correct our attitudes, and act as we should.

(16:13) ... **At This point, 3 People have made serious mistakes:**

- Sarai, took matters into her own hands.
- Abram, went along, but then refused to solve the problem.
- Hagar, ran away from her problem.

Sarai and Abram still received the son they wanted, and God solved Hagar's problem despite Abram's refusal to get involved. No problem is too big for God, if we are willing to let him help you.

*EL ROI
the God Who Sees me*

The Covenant of Circumcision
GENESIS 17:1-27

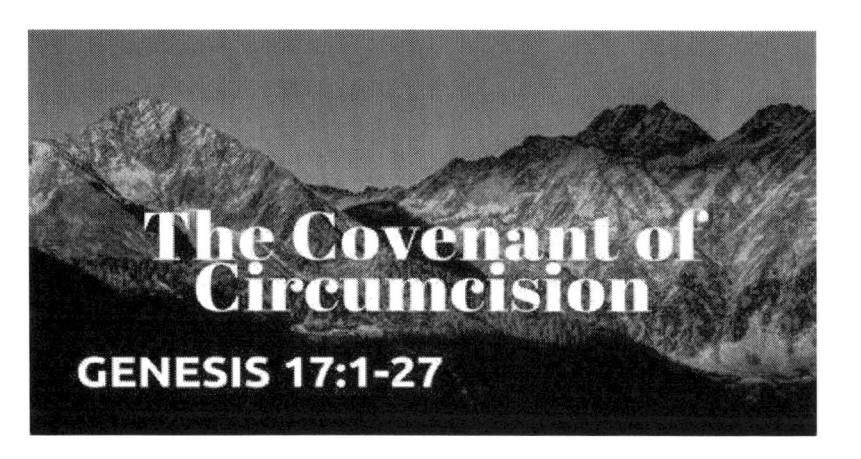

(17:5—14) ... God was making a covenant, between him and Abram. The terms were: Abram obey God and circumcise all males in his house, then God would give Abram heirs, property, power, and wealth. When we become part of God's covenant family, the blessings we receive far outweigh what we must give up.

(17:9,10) ... **Why did God require circumcision?**

- Sign of obedience to him in all matters
- Sign of belonging to his covenant people
- A symbol of "cutting off" the old life of sin, purifying one's heart, and dedicating oneself to God.
- Possibly as a health measure

Circumcision more than any other practice separated God's people from their heathen neighbors. In Abraham's day, this was essential to develop the pure worship of the one true God.

(Acts 7:8) ... And he gave him the covenant of circumcision: and so Abraham begat Isaac, and circumcised him the eighth day; and Isaac begat Jacob; and Jacob begat the twelve patriarchs.

(Deut 10:16) ... Circumcise therefore the foreskin of your heart, and be no more stiff-necked.

(17:17—27) ... Abraham, the man God considered righteous because of his faith, had trouble believing God's promise to him. Despite his doubts, however, he followed God's commands (17:22—27). Even people of great faith may have doubts. Focus on God's commitment to fulfill his promises to you, and then continue to obey.

(17:20) ... God did not forget Ishmael. Although he was not to be Abraham's heir, he would also be the father of a great nation. Regardless of your circumstances, God has not forgotten you. Obey him and trust in his plan.

(18:2—5) … Abraham was eager to show hospitality to these men, as was Lot (19:2). In Abraham's day, a person's reputation was largely connected to his hospitality—sharing of home and food. Even strangers were to be treated as highly honored guests. Hebrews 13:2 suggests that we, like Abraham, might actually entertain angels. We should think on this, next time we have an opportunity to meet a stranger need.

Gen 18:13-14

And the Lord said unto Abraham, Wherefore did Sarah laugh, saying, Shall I of a surety bear a child, which am old? ¹⁴Is any thing too hard for the Lord? At the time appointed I will return unto thee, according to the time of life, and Sarah shall have a son.

(18:14) … "Is anything too hard for the Lord?" "of course not!" Make it a habit to insert your specific need into the question. Asking reminds you that God is personally involved in your life and nudges you to ask for his power to help you.

(18:15) ... Sarah lied because she was afraid to be discovered. Fear is the most common motive for lying. We are afraid we will be exposed. Lying caused greater complications and more problems. If God can't be trusted with our innermost thoughts and fears, we are in great trouble.

(18:20-33) ... Did Abraham change God's mind? More likely, that God changed Abraham's mind. Abraham knew God was just and punishes sin, but may have wondered about God's mercy. Abraham was seeing how merciful God was. Abraham left conversation, knowing God was both fair and kind. Our prayers may not change God's mind, but may change ours, like it did with Abraham. Prayer is how we ca better comprehend God's mind. Abraham knew God must punish sin, but also knew God can be merciful to sinners. God knew there was not 10 righteous people in Sodom, but by mercy allowed Abraham to intercede. And by mercy willing to help Lot, before he destroyed Sodom, but he must punish sin. We should be thankful that God extends mercy to us.

(18:25) ... **God's fairness stood out.**

- Agree to spare the city for 10 righteous men.
- Showed great mercy to Lot

Showed great patience towards Lot, almost having to force him to leave Sodom. Even the godliest person deserves his justice.

(18:33) ... God showed Abraham that asking for anything is ok, with understanding, that God's answers come from his perspective. They are not always in harmony with ours, for he knows the whole story.

Genesis
Chapters 19-20

(19:1) ... The city gate was the meeting place for city officials and other men to discuss current events and transact business. A place of authority and status. The angels found Lot at the city gate, maybe his status in Sodom is a reason he was reluctant to leave (19:16; 18—22).

(19:5) ... The phrase "that we may know them" means the men wanted to have sex with Lot's guests.

    Judges 19:22 ... Now as they were making their hearts merry, behold, the men of the city, certain sons of Belial, beset the house round about, and beat at the door, and spake to the master of the house, the old man, saying, bring forth the man that came into thine house, that we may know him.

(19:8) ... How could any father give his daughters to be ravished by a mob of perverts, just to protect 2 strangers? Even though it was custom to protect guests, this showed hos bad sin had been absorbed into Lot's life.

    Deut 23:17 ... There shall be no whore of the daughters of Israel, nor a sodomite of the sons of Israel.

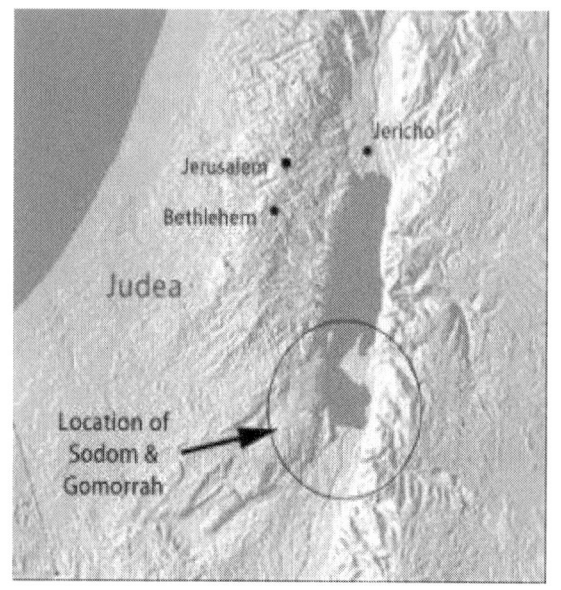

(19:13) ... God promised to spare Sodom, if 10 godly people were there (18:32). It is now widely thought that the buried city lies beneath the water of the Southern end of the Dead Sea.

Jude 1:7 ... Even as Sodom and Gomorrah, and the cities about them in like manner, giving themselves over to fornication, and going after strange flesh, are set forth for an example, suffering the vengeance of eternal fire.

(19:14) ... Lot lived amongst the ungodly for so long, that he wasn't a good witness for God. Does people see you as a witness for God? When he finally made a stand for God, no one listened. To make a difference, you must 1st decide to be different in your faith and conduct.

(19:16,29) ... Lot hesitated, and the angel seized his hand and rushed him to safety. He did not want to abandon the wealth and comfort he enjoyed in Sodom.

Notice how God's mercy toward Abraham extended to Lot and his family. Because Abraham pleaded for Lot, God was merciful and saved Lot, A righteous person can affect others for the good. James 5:16 says, "Confess your faults one to another, and pray one for another, that ye may be healed. The effectual fervent prayer of a righteous man availeth much.

(19:26) ... Lot's wife turned back to look at Sodom on fire. She was unwilling to turn completely from sin. You can't make progress with God, as long as you are holding on to the pieces of your old life. Matt 6:24, Jesus says you can't serve 2 masters.

(19:30-38) ... In this pitiful sequel to the destruction of Sodom, we see 2 women compelled to preserve their family line. They were driven by desperation—they feared they would never marry. Lot should have found good partners for his daughters. Perhaps the consequences of their action—Moab and Ammon became enemies of Israel—was God's way of judging their sin.

(19:37,38) ... Moab and Ben-Ammi were the products of incest. They became the fathers of Moabites and Ammonites, 2 of Israel's greatest enemies. Because of the family connection Moses was forbidden to attack them (Deut 2:9). Ruth the great-grandmother of David and an ancestor of Jesus, was from Moab.

Abraham & Abimelech
Genesis 20

(20:2) ... Although Abraham is one of our heroes of faith, he did not learn his lesson well enough the 1st time. In fact, by giving into temptation again, he risked turning a sinful act into a sinful pattern of lying when he felt his life was in danger. No matter how much we love God, certain temptations are especially difficult to resist. These are the vulnerable spots in our spiritual armor. God is watching out for us, when we struggle with these weaknesses.

(20:6) ... Abimelech had unknowingly taken a married woman to be his wife and was about to commit adultery. But God somehow prevented him from touching Sarah and held him back from sinning. How many times has God done the same for us, holding us back from sin in ways we can't even detect?

(20:11-13) ... Because Abraham mistakenly assumed that Abimelech was a wicked man, he made a quick decision to tell a ½ truth. He thought it was more effective to deceive Abimelech instead of trusting God. Don't assume God will not work in a situation that has potential problems.

Why did God punish Abimelech, when he has no idea Sarah was married?

- Even thou Abimelech had good intentions, if Sarah was living there, he was in danger of sinning.
- Punishment of "closing up all wombs in the house" was only for the time Sarah was there, and the temptation of sin.
- The punishment showed that Abraham was in league with a powerful God. This may have made Abimelech to respect + fear Abraham's God.

THE BIRTH OF... WAIT FOR IT... ISAAC!
GENESIS 21

(21:7) ... After repeated promises, a visit by 2 angels, and the appearance of the Lord himself, Sarah finally cried out with surprise and joy at the birth of her son. Because of her doubt, worry, and fear she had forfeited the peace she could have felt in God's promise to her.

God's Promise to Hagar

- Genesis 21:15-21
  - Out of water, Hagar starts to cry. God hears her cry and visits her with an angel.
  - 'Lift the boy up and take him by the hand, for I will make him into a great nation.'
  - 'God was with the boy as he grew up. He lived in the desert and became an archer. While he was living in the desert of Paran, his mother got him a wife from Egypt.'

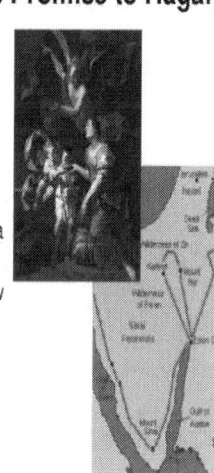

(21:18) ... Ismael became a ruler of a large tribe or nation. The Ishmaelites were nomads living in the wilderness of Sinai and Paran, south of Israel. One of Ishmael's daughters married Esau, Ismael's nephew (28:9). The Ishmaelites were hostile to Israel and God (Ps 83:5,6).

(21:31) ... Beersheba, southernmost city of Israel, lay on the edge of vast wilderness, from Egypt to the southwest and Mount Sinai to the South. The Southern portion had many wells and may be why Abraham settled there. Beersheba was also the home of Isaac.

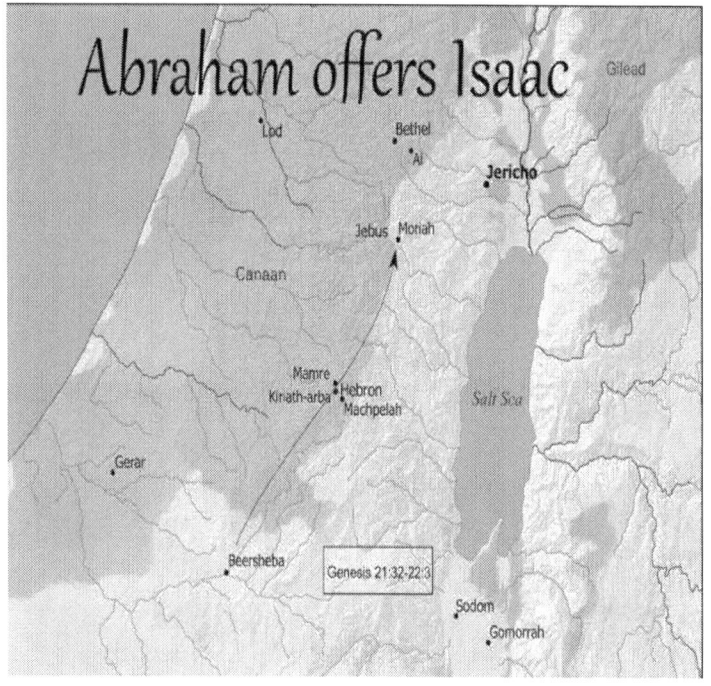

Abraham offers Isaac

Abraham + Isaac traveled 50-60 miles to Mount Moriah in 3 days. This was a difficult time for Abraham, who was on is way to sacrifice his beloved son, Issac.

(22:1) ... The word *tempt,* in this context, means "test". God gave Abraham a test, to deepen his capacity to obey God and develop his character. Just as fire refines ore to extract precious metals, God refines us through difficult circumstances. When this happens, we should see how God is stretching us to develop our character.

(22:3) ... That morning Abraham began one of the greatest acts of obedience in recorded history. Over the years he learned many lessons on obeying God. This time his obedience was prompted and complete. We should not expect our obedience to God to be easy or to come naturally.

(22:7,8) ... Why did God ask Abraham to perform human sacrifice? The heathen nations did this. God didn't want him to kill him physically, but to sacrifice Isaac in his heart, so it would be clearer that he loved God more than his promised son. God did this to strengthen his character and deepen his commitment to God. He also learned God will provide. We should realize this as well.

I drew this picture- 1/7/24

(22:13) ... Notice the parallel to the ram offered on the alter as a substitute for Issac and Christ offered on the cross, as a substitute, for us. Whereas God stopped Abraham from sacrificing his son, God did not, because if he did the rest of mankind would have died.

(22:15—18) ... **Abundant blessings Abraham received:**

- God gave his descendants the ability to conquer their enemies.
- God promised to bless Abraham's children and grandchildren who would in turn bless the whole earth.

Most often we think of blessings as gifts to be enjoyed, but when God blesses us, his blessings are intended to overflow onto others.

(23:1—4) ... In Abraham's day, death and burial were steeped in ritual and traditions. Failing to honor a dead person demonstrated the greatest lack of respect. Improper burial was equivalent to a curse. Mourning was an essential part. Since there were not funeral homes, friends and relatives helped prepared the body for burial, usually the same day because of the warm climate.

(23:4—6) ... Abraham was in a foreign land looking for a place to bury his wife. Strangers offered to help him because he was "a mighty prince" and they respected him. Those who invest their time and money in serving God often earn a pleasant return on their investment—a good reputation and the respect for others.

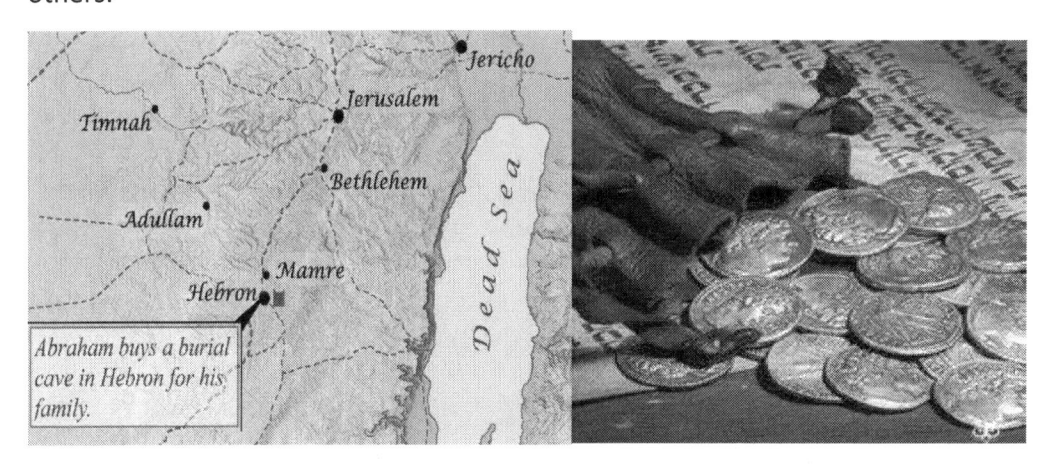

Abraham buys a burial cave in Hebron for his family.

(23:10—16) ... Ephron graciously offered to give the land to Abraham at no charge; Abraham insisted on paying for it. Abraham paid 400 shekels of silver for it. This was a high priest for the property. The custom was asking double the fair value, knowing buyer would ask for ½ price. Abraham did not bargain. Even though the land was promised to Abraham, he didn't just take it from Ephron.

A Bride for Isaac
Genesis 24

Abraham's Servant Finds Isaac a Wife

(24:4) ... Abraham wanted Isaac to marry within the family, common and accepted practice at the time, advantage of not being intermarriage with heathen neighbors. Son's wife was usually chosen by the parents.

(24:9) ... In Abraham's culture, this was how an agreement was sealed. Same as a handshake today or signed documents on the presence of a notary.

(24:11—14) ... The well, main source of water for the village, was usually located on the road outside of the town. Many had to walk a mile more for water. They could only use what they could carry home. Rebekah would have used the well 2x a day for her family. Abraham's servant asked God for guidance in this very important task. Be like Eliezar, asking God for guidance before any venture. Eliezar was simply asking God to show him a woman with an attitude of service- goes beyond the expected. He knew the importance of having the right heart, and asked God to help him with this task.

Profile of a true servant—via Eliezar

Accepted the Challenge	24:3,9
Examined Alternatives	24:5
Promised to Follow Directions	24:9
Made a Plan	24:12—14
Summited Plan to God	24:12—14
Prayed for Guidance	24:12—14
Devised a Strategy with room for God to Operate	24:12—14
Waited	24:21
Watched Carefully	24:21
Accepted the Answer Thankfully	24:26
Explained the situation to the Parties	24:34—49
Refused Unnecessary Delay	24:56
Followed through Entire Plan	24:66

REBEKAH

Some people are initiators, they help get the ball rolling. Rebekah would easily stand out in this group. Her life was characterized by the initiative, when she saw a need, she took action, even though the actions wasn't always right.

It was her initiative that 1st caught Eliezar's attention, the servant Abraham sent to find a wife for Isaac. It was common courtesy to give a drink to a stranger, but it took added character to also fetch water for 10 thirsty camels. Later after hearing the details of Eliezar's mission, Rebekah was immediately willing to be Isaac's bride.

Rebekah was aware that God's plan would be channeled through Jacob, not Esau (Gen 25:23). Not only did Jacob become her favorite, she actually planned ways to ensure that he would overshadow his older twin. Meanwhile, Isaac preferred Esau. This created conflict in their marriage. Rebekah felt justified in deceiving her husband, when it came to blessing the sons, and her ingenious plan was carried out to perfection.

Most of the time we try to justify the things we choose to do. Often, we attempt to add God's approval to our actions. We are responsible for what we do and must always be cautious about our motives. Initiative and action are admirable and right when they are controlled by God's wisdom.

Rebekah's Strengths and Accomplishments

- When confronted with a need she took immediate action.
- She was accomplishment oriented.

Rebekah's Weaknesses and Mistakes

- Her initiative was not always balanced with wisdom.
- She favored one of her sons.
- She deceived her husband.

Lessons from Rebekah's Life

- Our actions must be guided by God's Word.
- God can make use of our mistakes in his plan.
- Parental favoritism hurts a family.

Vital Statistics

- WHERE: Haran and Canaan
- OCCUPATION: Wife, mother, and household manager
- RELATIVES: Grandparents ➔ Nahor + Milcah
  Father ➔ Bethuel
  Husband ➔ Isaac
  Brother ➔ Laban
  Twin sons ➔ Esau + Jacob

ESAU

Common sense isn't all that common. Amen!!! Esau's life was filled with choices he must have regretted bitterly. He appears to have been a person who found it hard to consider consequences, reacting to the need of the moment without realizing what he was giving up to meet that need. Trading his birthright, for a pot of stew, was the clearest example of this weakness. He also chose wives in the direct opposition to his parent's wishes. He learned the hard way.

What are you willing to trade for the things you want? Does your family, spouse, integrity, body, or soul get included in these deals? Your greatest need is to find afocal point other than "What I need now." The only worthy focal point is God. A relationship with him will not only give an ultimate purpose to your life; it will also be a daily guideline for living. Meet him in the pages of the Bible.

Esau's Strength and Accomplishments

- Ancestor of the Edomites
- Known for his archery skills
- Able to forgive after explosive anger

Esau's Weaknesses and Mistakes

- In important decisions tends to choose immediate need, rather than, long-term effect.
- Angered parents by poor marriage choice.

Lessons from Esau's Life

- God allows certain events in our lives to accomplish his overall purposes, but we are still responsible for our actions.
- Consequences are important to consider.
- It is possible to have a great anger and yet not sin.

Vital Statistics

- WHERE: Canaan
- OCCUPATION: Herdsman + skillful hunter
- RELATIVES: Parents ➔ Isaac + Rebekah
    Twin brother ➔ Jacob
        Wives ➔ Judith + Basemath + Mahalath
        Kids ➔ Eliphaz + Reuel + Jeush + Korah + Jaalam

JACOB

Abraham, Isaac, and Jacob are among the most significant people in the Old Testament. It is important to realize that this significance is not based upon their personal characters, but upon the character of God. They are all men who earned the respect and even peer of their peers. They were wealthy and powerful, yet capable of lying, deceit, and selfishness. They were not perfect heroes; instead, they were like us, trying to please God, but often falling short. Jacob was the 3rd link in God's plan to start a nation from Abraham. Before Jacob was born, God promised that his plan would be worked out through Jacob and not his twin brother Esau. Although Jacob's methods were not always respectful, his skill, determination, and patience have to be admired. Jacob's life had 4 stages.

The 4 stages of Jacob's Life:

1. Jacob lived up to his name, which means "One who supplants," "undermines or grabs." He grabbed Esau's heel at birth, and by the time he fled from home, he grabbed his brother's birthright and blessing as well. During his flight, God 1st appeared to him. God awakened in Jacob a personal knowledge of himself.
2. Jacob experienced life from the other side, being manipulated and deceived by Laban. But there is a curious change: Jacob of stage 1 would have left Laban, but now after deciding to leave, waited 6 years for God's permission.
3. Jacob was in a new role as a grabber. This time, by the Jordan River, he grabbed on to God and wouldn't let go. He realized his dependence on the God who had continued to bless him. This relationship became essential and names changed to Israel, "A prince who prevails with God."
4. Last stage, he was grabbed by God; in responding to Joseph's invitation to come to Egypt, Jacob waited until he had God's approval"

Jacob's Strengths and Accomplishments

- Father of the 12 tribes of Israel
- 3rd in Abrahamic line of God's plan
- Determined and worked hard for what he wanted.
- Good businessman

Jacob's Weaknesses and Mistakes

- Faced with conflict, relied on himself instead of God
- Tend to accumulate wealth for himself

Lessons from Jacob's Life

- Security doesn't lie in the amount of goods.
- All good and bad intentions are woven by God into his ongoing plan.

Vital Statistics

- WHERE: Canaan, married and started a family in Haran, moved to Egypt
- OCCUPATION: Shepherd + livestock owner
- RELATIVES: Parents → Issac + Rebekah   Twin Brother → Esau
            Father-in-Law → Laban   Wives → Rachel + Leah
                Sons → Reuben … Dan   Daughter → Dinah
                    Simeon … Naphtali
                (Ephraim) Levi … Gad
                    Judah … Asher
                    Issachar … Joseph (Manasseh)
                    Zebulun … Benjamin

(24:15,16) … Rebekah had physical beauty, but the servant was looking for a sign of inner beauty. How do we develop inner beauty? Patience, kindness, and joy are the beauty treatments that help us become truly lovely—on the inside.

(24:18—20) … Rebeka's servant heart was clearly demonstrated as she willingly and quickly drew water for Eliezar and his camels. The pots were large and heavy. It would take up to 25 gallons per camel after a week's travel. Eliezar knew she was a woman who went more than the minimum.

(24:26-27) … Eliezar thanked God for his goodness and guidance. Our 1st response to God, using and leading us, should always be praise and thanksgiving, that he would choose to work through us.

(24:42-48) … When Eliezar told his story to Laban, he spoke openly of God and his goodness. Often, we're afraid that we will be misunderstood, rejected, or seen as "too religious". Instead, we should share openly what God is doing in our lives.

(24:60-65) … "Let thy seed possess the gate of those which hated them" could be translated "May you overcome all your enemies." When Rebekah knew the man coming to greet her was Issac, husband-to-be, she followed custom, by demounting from her camel, and placed a veil over her face as a bride.

(25:21) ... As Issac pleaded with God for children, the Bible tells is to plead for our important requests.

As Isaac realized, God may withhold for a while, because:

1. He wants to deepen out insight into what we really need.
2. He wants to broaden out appreciation for his answer.
3. He wants to allow us to mature so we can use gifts more wisely.

(25:31—33) ... A birthright was a special honor given to the 1st born son, that included a double portion of the family inheritance, along with the honor of one day becoming the family leader. The oldest could sell or give away his birthright, but would lose material goods and his leadership. By trading it, Esau showed complete disregard for the spiritual blessings that would have come his way. He traded it for immediate pleasure of food. He acted on impulse, without thinking of long-range consequences. We can avoid making Esau's mistake by comparing the short-term satisfaction with the long-term consequences before we act. Esau exaggerated his hunger, stating he was about to die. The desire of the moment distorted his perspective. Getting through that pressure-filled but short moment is often the hardest part of overcoming temptation.

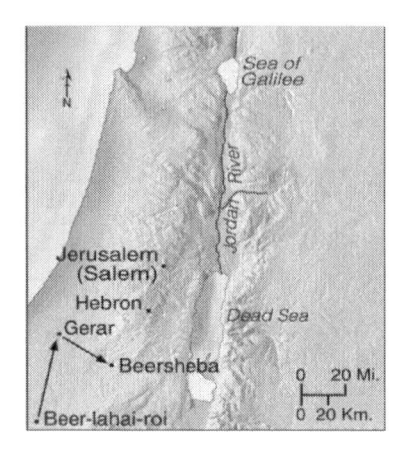

Isaac had settled near Beer-Lahai-Roi ("the well Lahai-Roi") where his sons, Jacob and Esau was born. A famine drove him to Gerar, but when he became wealthy, his jealous neighbors asked him to leave. From Gerar he moved to Beer-Sheba.

(26:1) ... The Philistine tribe would become a fierce enemy to Israel. Philistine means "sea people" originally sailors from the Mediterranean Sea, lived on the southwest coast, few but ferocious in battle. They were nice to Isaac, but would plague Israel during the time of Joshua, the judges, and David.

(26:7—18) ... Isaac was afraid that the men in Gerar would kill him and Rebekah. So, he lied claiming she was his sister. Eventually he knew about the actions of his father Abraham (12:10—13) and (20:1—5). Parents help shape the world's future by the way they shape their children's values. What kind of example are you setting for your children?

God kept his promise to bless Isaac. The neighboring Philistines grew jealous because everything Isaac did seemed to go right. So, they plugged his wells to get back at him. Jealousy will tear apart the mightiest of nations or the closest friends. You should thank God for other's fortune. The desolate Gerar was located on the edge of a wilderness. Water was precious as gold. To "Stop" or plug up someone's well was an act of war. Isaac had every right to fight back, but he chose to keep the peace. In the end the Philistines respected him for his patience.

ARE YOUR WELLS PLUGGED UP?

Text: Genesis 26:12-22

(26:17—22) ... 3 times Isaac and his men dug new wells. When the 1st two disputes arose, Isaac moved on. Finally, there was no room for everyone. Rather than starting a fight, Isaac chose peace. Ask God for wisdom on when to withdraw and when to stand and fight.

Isa 54:2 ... Enlarge the place of thy tent, and let them stretch forth the curtains of thine habitations: spare not, lengthen thy cords, and strengthen thy stakes;

(26:26—31) ... With his enemies wanting to make peace, Isaac was quick to respond, turning the occasion into celebration. We should be just as receptive to those who want to patch things up with us. When God's influence in our lives begins to attract people—even enemies—we must take that opportunity to reach out to them with God's love.

Esau's Wives

(26:34,35) ... Esau married heathen woman, and this upset his parents greatly. Most parents have a lifetime of insight into their children's character. You may not agree with everything your parents say, but at least talk with them and listen carefully. This will help avoid hard feelings Esau experienced.

(27:5—10) ... When Rebekah learned that Isaac was about to bless Esau, she quickly devised a plan to trick him into blessing Jacob instead. God already told her that Jacob was going to become the family leader, but she took matters into her own hands. She tried to do something wrong to try and bring what God said would happen. No matter how good we think our goals are, we should not try and achieve them unjustly. Would God approve of the methods you are using to accomplish your goals?

(27:11—13) ... How we react to a moral dilemma often exposes our real motives. Frequently we are more worried about getting caught than about doing what's right. Jacob did not seem concerned about the deceitfulness of his mom's plan; instead, he was afraid of getting caught. If this is you in a situation, let your fear of getting caught be a warning to do right. Jacob paid a high price for carrying out his dishonest plan.

    Jacob hesitated when he heard the plan, even though he questioned, for the wrong reason, he protested which gave her a 2nd chance to reconsider. Rebekah was so wrapped up in the plan, that she couldn't see clearly. Sin had trapped her and was degrading her character. Correcting yourself in the middle of doing wrong can bring hurt and disappointment, but it also brings freedom from sins control.

(27:19) ... **Jacob's consequences for deceiving Isaac:**

1. He never saw his mother again.
2. His brother wanted to kill him.
3. He was deceived by his uncle, Laban.
4. His family became torn by strife.
5. Esau became the founder of an enemy nation.
6. He was exile from family for years

Imagine how different his life would have been had he and his mother allowed God to do things his way, in his time?

(27:33—37) ... In ancient times, a person's word was binding (like a written contract today), especially when it was a formal oath. This is why Issac's blessing was irrevocable. Before Isaac died, he performed a ceremony of blessings, were he officially handed over the birthright to the rightful heir. It wasn't official until the blessing was pronounced and after it was given, the birthright could not be taken away. Although Jacob had been given his birthright by Esau years before, he still needed his father's blessing to make it binding.

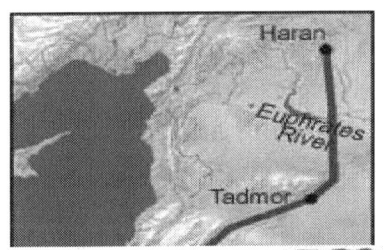

After deceiving Esau, Jacob ran for his life, traveling more than 400 miles to Haran where an uncle, Laban lived. In Haran, Jacob married and started a family.

(27:41) ... Esau was so angry at Jacob that he failed to see his own wrong in giving his birthright away. Jealous anger pollutes clear thinking by binding us to the good things we have and making us dwell on what we don't have. Esau wanted to kill Jacob. When you lose something of great value, anger is the 1st and natural reaction.

You can control your feelings of anger:

1. By recognizing your reaction for what it is.
2. By praying for strength.

By asking God for help to see the opportunities that even your bad situation may provide

THE STORY OF JACOB ... (28:10—36:43)

Jacob did everything, both right and wrong, with great zeal. His deceived his brother Esau and his father Isaac. He wrestled with an angel and worked 14 years to marry a woman he loved. Through Jacob we learn how a strong leader can also be a servant. We also see how wrong action can turn around on us.

(28:9) ... Ishmael was Isaac's ½ brother, the son of Abraham and Hagar, Sarah's servant girl (16:1—4,15). After marring 2 foreign girls, Esau hoped his marriage into Ishmael's family would please his parents, Isaac and Rebekah.

Gen 36:2,3 ... Esau took his wives of the daughters of Canaan; Adah the daughter of Elon the Hittite, and Aholibamah the daughter of Anah the daughter of Zibeon the Hivite; And Bashemath Ishmael's daughter, sister of Nebajoth.

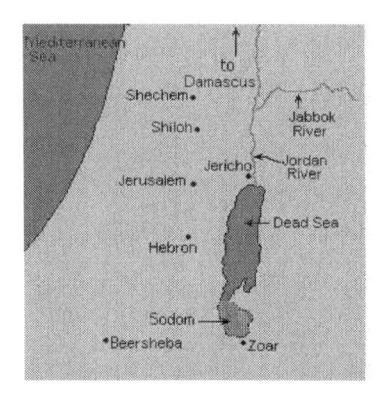

(28:10—15) ... God's covenant promised to Abraham and Isaac was offered to Jacob as well. Jacob had to develop his own relationship with God. He couldn't use his father's relationship with God, because he has no grand-children. It's not enough to hear Bible stories from your family you have to become part of the story yourself (Gal 3:6,7)

(28:19) ... Bethel was about 10 miles north of Jerusalem bad 60 miles north of Beersheba, where Jacob left his family. This was where Abraham made 1 of his 1st sacrifices to God. Later Bethel became the center of idol worship, and the prophet Hosea condemned its evil practices.

RACHEL

History seems to repent itself. 2x's a town well at Haran was a site of significant events in one family's story. It's where Rebekah met Eliezer, who come to find a wife for Issac. Years later Rebekah's son Jacob returned the favor by serving his cousin Rachel and her sheep from the same well. This developing relationship teaches us both patience and love.

Jacob had the patience to wait 7 years for her but kept busy in the meantime. His commitment to her kindled a story loyalty within Rachel. Her loyalty to Jacob got out of hand and became self-destructive. She was frustrated by her barrenness and desperate to compete with her sister for Jacob's attention.

We can, like Rachel, trying somehow to earn love—God's love. What happens is we think we've been good enough to deserve his love or we realize we can't earn his love and assume that it's not ours. Th Bible shouts loudly, that God loves us! His love has no beginning (he is love) and is incredibly patient. God wants us to live because of his love. Respond to him; love him with your whole being; giving yourself to him in thanksgiving, not as a payment. Live life fully, in the freedom of knowing you are loved.

Rachel's Strengths and Accomplishments

- She showed loyalty to her family.
- She mothered Joseph and Benjamin after being barren for years.

Rachel's Weaknesses and Mistakes

- Her envy and competitiveness marred her relationship with her sister Leah.
- She was capable of dishonesty when she took her loyalty too far.
- She failed to realize that Jacob's devotion was not dependent on her ability to have children.

Lessons from Rachel's life

- Loyalty must be controlled by what is true and right.
- Love is accepted and not earned.

Vital Statistics

- WHERE: Haran
- OCCUPATION: Shepherdess, wife, mother, and household manager.
- RELATIVES: Father → Laban   Aunt → Rebekah
  Sister → Leah
  Husband → Jacob
  Sons → Joseph and Benjamin

Gen 29:20 … "And Jacob served seven years for Rachel; and they seemed unto him but a few days, for the love he had to her."

LEAH

Women in her day were considered property. Daughters were traded in business deals. Her dad, Laban, gave her to a man that didn't love her, but God loved her. Laban tricked Jacob into marring her, by then excusing it to customs, that oldest daughters had to married 1st. Although Leah was not his 1st choice, he accepted her as his wife.

Leah revealed how she felt about Jacob, in the name of her 1st son, Reuben. The names expressed her desire to be noticed by her husband. There was constant friction between her and her sister, Rachel, for Jacob's attention. They measured their worth against each other by their ability to bear children. Leah won the contest. Rachel died bearing 2 sons. This victory carried little satisfaction. The greatest honor Jacob gave Leah, was to bury her with his parents and grand-parents in the cave of Machpelah (49:31).

Although God loved Leah, we are not told of her response to him. Her inability to appreciate God's love also made her unable to love others. When we struggle to love others, we can be helped by reflecting on the fact that God loves us. If God's love doesn't free us, we need to think again.

Leah's Strength and Accomplishments

- She bore Jacob 6 sons and 1 daughter.
- She worked with Jacob and Rachel to outwit Laban's manipulation.

Leah's Weaknesses and Mistakes

- She envied her sister over Jacob's love.
- She competed with Rachel for Jacob's attention and respect.
- Opportunities for joy can be missed through wrong motives.

Vital Statistics

- WHERE: Padan Aram
- OCCUPATION: Wife and mother
- RELATIVES: Father ➔ Laban   Husband ➔ Jacob
             Daughter ➔ Dinah
                Sons ➔ Reuben
                       Simeon
                       Levi
                       Judah
                       Issachar
                       Zebulun

LABAN

Laban's whole life was stamped by self-centeredness. His goal was to look out for himself. He made profitable arrangements for his sister Rebekah's marriage to Isaac and used his daughters lives as bargaining chips. Jacob eventually outmaneuvered Laban, but he was not willing to admit defeat. But he did realize that Jacob and Jacob's God were more than he could handle. Do you act in self-centered and selfish motives? Do you willingly admit when you are wrong? Recognizing selfishness is painful, but it is the 1st step on the road back to God.

Laban's Strengths and Accomplishments

- He controlled 2 generations of marriages in the Abrahamic family.
- He was quick-witted.

Laban's Weaknesses and Mistakes

- He manipulated others for his own benefit.
- He was unwilling to admit wrongdoing.
- He benefited financially by using Jacob but never got benefited spiritually by knowing and worshipping Jacob's God.

Lessons from Laban's Life

- Those who use people usually get used.
- God's plan can't be blocked.

Vital Statistics

- WHERE: Haran
- OCCUPATION: Wealthy sheep breeder
- RELATIVES: Father ➔ Bethuel   Sister ➔ Rebekah
    Brother-in-law ➔ Isaac
        Daughters ➔ Rachel and Leah
        Son-in-law ➔ Jacob

Genesis 29

- **Jacob comes to the well of Haran**
- **Jacob meets Rachel by the well**
- **Arrangements made for Rachel to be Jacob's bride**
- **Jacob gets two wives Rachel and Leah**

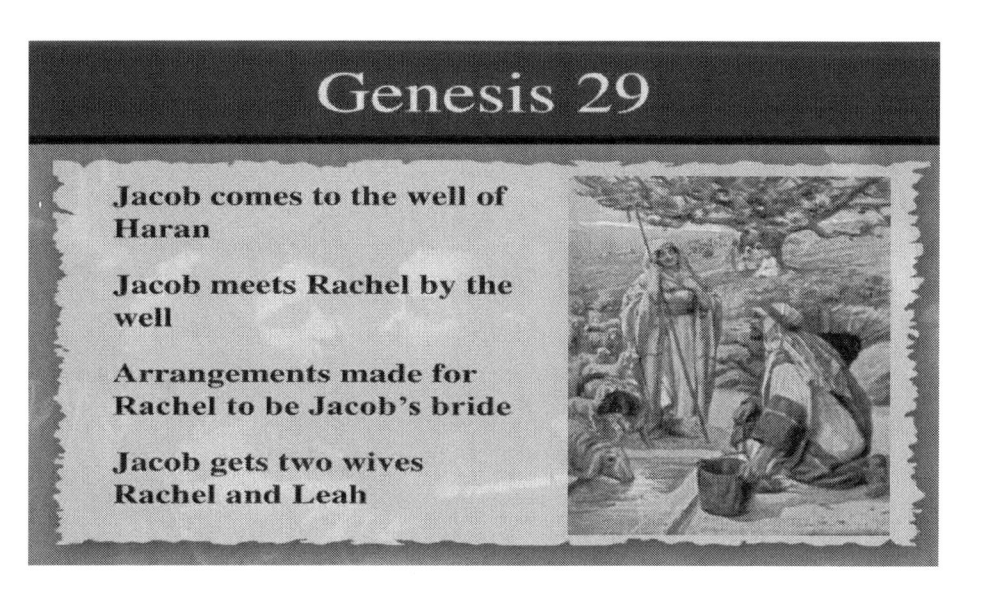

(29:18—27) ... It was custom for a man to present a dowry (gift) to the family of his future wife. To compensate for the loss of the daughter. Jacob had no material gift to offer, so he agreed to work for 7 years for Laban. There was another custom Laban didn't tell Jacob. The other daughter had to be married 1st. By giving him Leah and not Rachel, Laban tricked him into working another 7 years.

(29:20—28) ... People wonder if waiting a long time for something is worth it. Jacob worked by total of 14 years for Rachel. The most important desires are worth working and waiting for. Patience is hardest when we need it most, but is the key to achieving our goals.

LABAN TRICKS JACOB

(29:23—35) ... Jacob flew into a rage when he learned that Laban had tricked him. The deceiver of Esau was now being deceived himself. It's easy to get mad at being wronged, but closing our eyes to the same wrong we have done to others. Sin has a way of coming back around to bite us. Although Jacob was tricked, he kept his part of the bargain. There was more at hand, than his hurt feelings. Nursing out wounds or plotting revenge makes us unable to see God's perspective.

(29:32) ... In Old Testament parents hoped their children would live up to their names. Sometimes a person's name was changed because their character and name didn't match. This happened to Jacob (one who supplants), was changed to Israel (a prince who prevails with God). His character had changed to the point he wasn't seen any longer as a deceiver, but as a God-honoring man.

(30:3) ... All 3 patriarchs (Abraham, Isaac, and Jacob) had wives who struggled to bear kids.

- Abraham has sex with Sarah's servant, introducing bitterness and jealousy into his family.
- Isaac prayed to God, when his wife was barren, God answered and she had twin sons.
- Jacob followed after his grand-father, Abraham's example and had children by his wives' servants, leading to sad and bitter consequences.

(30:4—12) ... Rachel and Leah were in a cruel contest. They both gave their servants to Jacob as concubines. It would have been wise to refuse, even though it was custom. You would be wise and spare much heartbreak if you look at the potential consequences, to you or others, of your actions. Are you doing anything now that might cause future problems.

(30:14) ... <u>Songs of Solomon 7:13</u> ... The mandrakes give a smell, and at our gates are all manner of pleasant fruits, new and old, which I have laid up for thee, O my beloved.

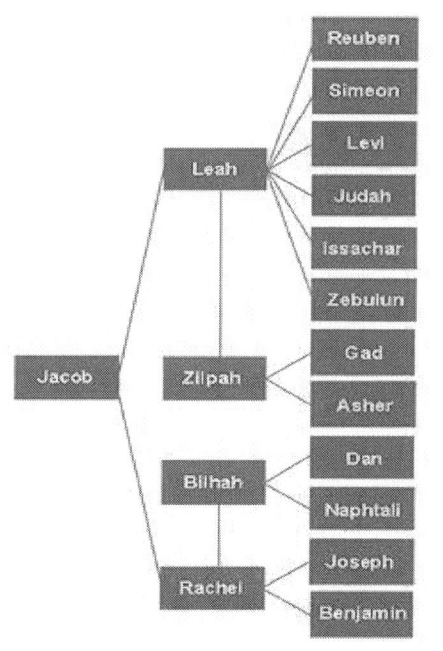

Jacob's many wives (2 wives—2 sub-wives) led to sad and bitter consequences among the children. Anger, resentment, and jealousy were common among Jacob's sons. It is interesting to note that the worst fighting and rivalry occurred between Leah's children, Rachel's children, and among the tribes that descended from them.

(30:22—24) ... The Lord finally answered Rachel's prayers and gave her a child of her own. In the meantime, she took matters in her own hands by giving her servant to Jacob. Trusting God when nothing seems to happen is difficult, but it is harder still to love with the consequences of taking matters into your own hands. Resist the temptation to think God has forgotten you. Have patience and courage to wait for God to act.

(31:1,2) ... Jacob's wealth made Laban's sons jealous. It is sometimes difficult to be happy when others are better than we are. To compare our success with that od others is a dangerous way to judge the quality of our lives. By comparing ourselves to others, we may be giving jealousy a foothold. We can avoid jealousy by rejoicing in other's success (Romans 12:15).

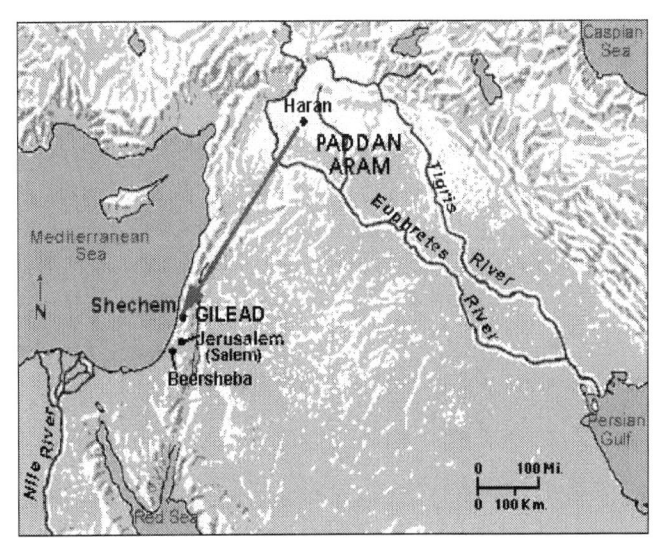

God told Jacob to leave Haran and return to his homeland. Jacob took his family, crossed the Euphrates River, and headed 1st for the land of Gilead. Laban caught up to him there.

(31:4—13) ... Although Laban treated Jacob unfairly, God still increased Jacob's prosperity. God's power is not limited by lack of fair play. He has the ability to meet our needs and make us thrive even though others mistreat us. To give in and respond unfairly in return is to be no different from your enemies.

(31:14—15) ... It wasn't difficult for Rachel and Leah to leave home because their father, Laban treated them poorly as well. Per custom, they were supposed to receive the benefits of the dowry Jacob paid for them, which was 14 years of work. When Laban didn't give them what was theirs, they knew they would never inherit anything from their father. So, they approved of Jacob's plan to take the wealth he gained and leave.

(31:19) ... Many people kept small wooden or metal idols in their homes, called teraphim, that they thought would protect the home and offer advice when needed. They had legal significance, when passed along, that person could rightfully claim the greatest part of the family's inheritance. No wonder Laban was concerned when it was missing (31:30).

(31:32) ... Can you remember feeling absolutely sure about something? Jacob was so sure that no one stole Laban's idol that he vowed to kill the offender. This statement put Rachel's safety in serious jeopardy. Even when you are confident and you're sure, it's best to not male rash statements. Someone may hold you to them.
(31:38—42) ... Jacob did more than was expected.

How does making a habit of doing more than expected payoff?

1. It pleases God.
2. Like Joseph, you can earn recognition and advancement.
3. It will enhance your reputation.
4. It builds other's confidence in you.
5. It gives you more experience and knowledge.
6. It will also develop your spiritual maturity.

(31:49) … To be binding, an agreement had to be witnesses by a 3rd party. In this case, Jacob and Laban, used God as their witness that they would keep their word.

(32:1) … Why did an angel of God meet Jacob? In the Bible, angels often intervened in human situations. Sometimes, they came in human form, these angels must have looked different, because Jacob recognized them. Not sure why they met Jacob, but he knew God was with him.

(32:3) … The last time Jacob seen his brother Esau; his brother wanted to kill him. Esau was so angry, that he vowed to kill Jacob, when their father died (27:41). Fearing the reunion, Jacob sent a messenger ahead with gifts. He hoped to buy Esau's favor.

(32:9—12) … Jacob was about to meet his brother for the 1st time in 20 years, and was frantic with fear. He collected his thought and began to pray.

(32:26) … Jacob continued this wrestling match all night just to be blessed. He was persistent. God encourages persistence in all areas of life, including spiritual. Where in your spiritual life do you need more persistence? Strong character results from struggling under though conditions.

(32:27—29) … God gave many people in the Bible new names (Abraham, Sarah, Peter, and Paul). Their names were now a symbol of how God changed their lives. Jere, Jacob, the ambitious deceiver, have now become Israel, the prince who struggles with God and prevails.

(33:1—11) … It is great to see Esau's change of heart. Esau was content with what he had. Jacob exclaims how great it is to see his brother pleased with him (33:10). Life can deal us bad situations. We can feel cheated as Esau did, but we don't have to remain bitter. We can remove bitterness by honestly expressing our feelings to God, forgiving those who have wronged us, and being content with what we have.

(33:3) … Bowing Low 7x's was a sign of respect given to a king. Jacob was taking every precaution as he met Esau, hoping to dispel any thoughts of revenge.

(33:4) ... Esau greeted Jacob with a great hug. Time away from each other allowed the bitter wounds to heal. They realized their relationship was more important than their real estate.

(33:11) ... **In the Bible gifts meant several things:**

- <u>As a bribe</u>: Esau refused the gift because he had forgiven Jacob and had wealth of his own.
- It could mean an expression of affection.
- It was a customary way of greeting someone before an important meeting.

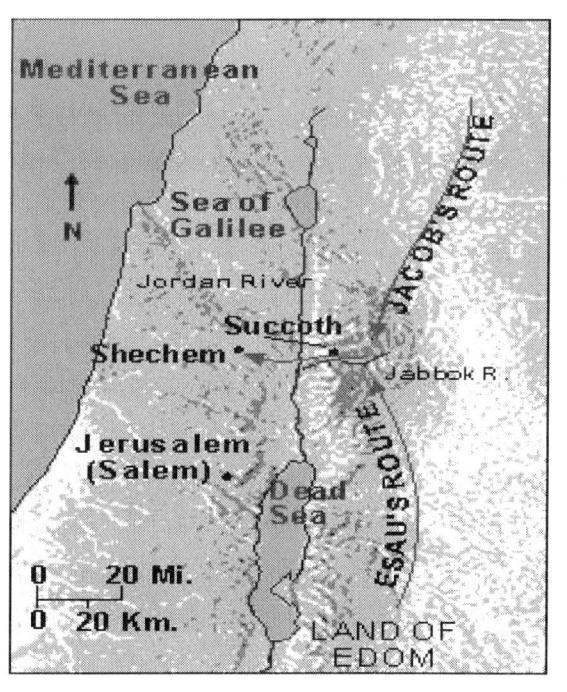

After a joyful reunion with Esau (who journeyed from Edom), Jacob set up camp in Succoth. Later he moved to Shechem where his daughter Dinah was raped and 2 sons took revenge on that city.

DINAH

She had 10 older and 2 younger brothers. Not sure how he bitterness and jealousy between her mom and aunt affecter the only girl-child in the family. By the time Dinah was a teenager, her family was living in Shechem, town north if Bethel and Jerusalem in the Promised Land.

    Nobody really paid much attention to Dinah until she walked in town one day. She was noticed and raped by Shechem, the son of the ruler of the city. Violated and shamed, Dinah found herself in the center of a family crisis. Shechem asked his father to arrange a marriage with Dinah. In Jacob and her brother's eyes, Dinah had been damaged and their family had been insulted. Jacob failed to provide any fatherly leadership and his sons took matters in their own hands. The result was treacherous and bloody.

    In this, the victim was overlooked. She was neither comforted or consulted. She was almost treated with as much disrespect by her family as Shechem. By handing her over to Shechem, they used Dinah as a bait in a trap that led to the murder of all the men in the village. Jacob was angry at his sins for what they did but did nothing.

    You probably know someone who can identify closely with Dinah. Perhaps you have experienced the same anonymity as a victim who was unnoticed or forgotten. Remember even when every forgets, God doesn't; when no one seems to notice, God sees; and when no one cares, God cares. Begin to see God today in prayer about your past.

Dinah's Strengths and Accomplishments

- Jacob's only daughter.

Lessons from Dinah's Life

- Thoughtless avengers often hurt original victims for a 2nd time.
- Family members can be trampled in the rush for family honor.

Vital Statistics

- WHERE: Padan Aram
- RELATIVES: Parents → Jacob + Leah
  Aunt → Rachel
  Grand-parents → Isaac + Rebekah + Laban
  Uncle → Esau
  Brothers → Reuben
  Simeon
  Levi
  Judah
  Issachar
  Zebulun
  Gad
  Asher
  Dan
  Naphtali
  Joseph
  Benjamin

(34:1—4) ... Shechem may have been a victim of "love at 1st sight", but his actions were impulsive and evil. The consequences of hos deeds were severe for his family and Jacob's (34:25—31). Don't allow sexual passion to boil over into evil actions. Passion must be controlled!

2 Sam 13:14 ... Howbeit he would not hearken unto her voice: but, being stronger than she, forced her, and lay with her.

(34:25—31) ... Why did Simeon and Levi take such harsh actions against the city of Shechem? God wanted Jacob's family to remain separate from their heathen neighbors. The brothers thought this meant better as well. This attitude led to the terrible slaughter of innocent people.

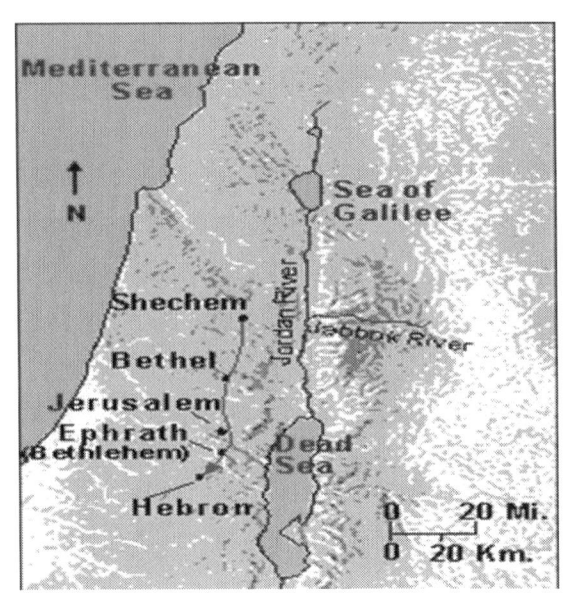

After Jacob's sons Simeon and Levi destroyed Shechem, God told Jacob to move to Bethel where God reminded him that his name changed it Israel. He then traveled to Hebron, but along the way his dear wife Rachel died near Ephrath (Bethlehem).

(34:30,31) ... In seeking revenge against Shechem, Simeon and Levi lied, stole, and murdered. Their wat of receiving justice was wrong. Because of their sin, their father cursed them with his dying breath (49:5—7). Generations later their descendants lost the part of the Promised Land allotted to them. When tempted, leave revenge to God.

(35:2) ... Sometimes idols were seen as good luck charm than gods. Some who believed in God still had them in their homes, as some Christians today has good luck charms. Jacob believed they should not be in his home. He wanted nothing to divert his family's spiritual focus. We should agree.

Jacob ordered his household to destroy all their idols. These idols in our lives can ruin our faith. An idol is anything we put before God. They can also be thoughts and desires. We should get rid of anything that could stand between us and God.

(35:4) ... In Jacob's day earrings were often worn as good luck charms to ward off evil. His family had to cleanse themselves of all heathen influences including reminders of foreign gods.

(35:10) ... Although Jacob's life was littered with difficulties and trials, his new name was a tribute to his desire to stay close to God despite life's appointments. As life gets tough, we should determine to prevail with God through life's storms. You can't prevail with God unless you have troubles to prevail over.

(35:13,14) ... Anointing oil was olive oil of the finest grade of purity. It was expensive, using it showed high value placed upon the anointed object. Jacob was showing great respect for the place where he met with God.

REUBEN

Jacob summarized the personality of his son, Reuben, as water. Except when frozen, water has no stable shape of its own. It always shapes itself to its container or environment. Reuben usually had good intentions, but seemed unable to stand against the crowd. This is why he was hard to trust. He went along with his brothers in their actions against Joseph, while hoping to counteract the evil in private. Plan failed. Reuben's sleeping with his father's concubine showed how little integrity he had left. How closely does Jacob's description of his son— "unstable as water "—describe your life?

Reuben's Strengths and Accomplishments

- Saved Joseph's life by taking the other brothers out of murder.
- Showed intense love for his father by offering his own

Reuben's Weaknesses and Mistakes

- Gave in quickly to group pressure. Slept with father's concubine.
- As oldest son, with the authority, did not directly protect Joseph.

Lessons from Reuben's Life

- Public and private integrity must be the same, one will destroy the other.
- Punishment for sin may not be immediate, but it is certain

Vital Statistics

- WHERE: Canaan and Egypt
- OCCUPATION: Shepherd
- RELATIVES: Parents ➔ Jacob + Leah
    Full brothers ➔ Simeon + Levi + Judah
    ½ brothers ➔ Gad + Asher + Issachar + Zebulun
        Joseph + Benjamin + Dan + Naphtali
    ½ sister ➔ Dinah
        Wife ➔ Eliuram (from the book of Jasher) ?
        Sons ➔ Hanoch + Phallu + Hezron + Carmi

(35:18) ... Ben-Oni means "Son of my sorrow". Benjamin means "Son of my right hand"

(35:22) ... Reuben's sin was costly, although not immediate. As oldest son he stood to receive a double portion of the family inheritance. On Jacob's deathbed, he assembled the family for the final blessings. Jacob took away Reubens double blessing because Reuben slept with Bilhah, Jacob's concubine. Our sin we thought we got away with, could be breeding serious consequences.

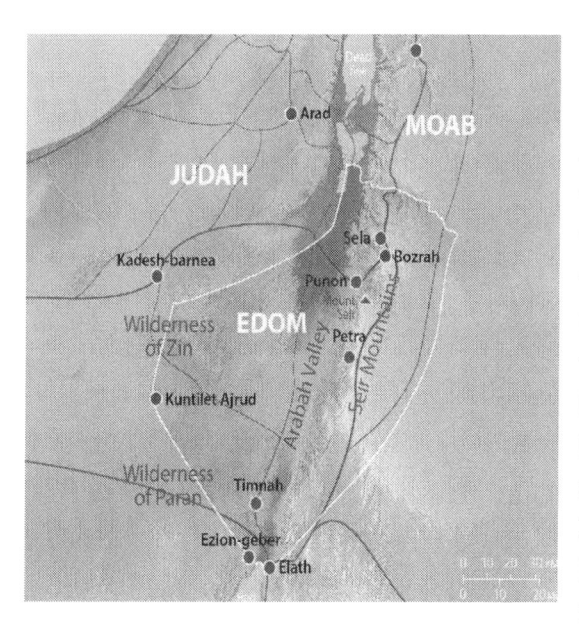

(36:9) ... The Edomites were descendants of Esau, who lived South and East of the Dead Sea. It was rugged mountains and desolate wilderness. Several major roads led through Edom, because it was rich in natural resources. Edom refused to let them enter the land, and later became bitter enemies of King David. Edom and Israel shared the same ancestor, Isaac, and the same border. Israel looked down on the Edomites because they inter-married the Canaanites.

(36:15) ... The title "duke" is equivalent to "head of clan".

JOSEPH

Joseph's natural self-assurance, increased by him being Jacob's favorite son and knowing God's design on his life, was unbearable to his 10 older brothers, who eventually conspired against him. But this quality about him is the very thing, that allowed him to survive and prosper where most would have failed. He added quiet wisdom to his confidence and won the hearts of everyone he met—Potiphar, the jailer, other prisoners, the king, and after many years those 10 brothers.

    He was betrayed and deserted by family, exposed to sexual temptation and punishment for doing the right thing; he endured a long imprisonment and forgotten by those he helped. Can you identify with Joesph on any of those hardships?

    Joseph's positive response to these hardships transformed each setback into a step forward. His approach was "What shall I do now?" instead of "Why?", everyone was aware that God was with him. There is nothing like God's presence to shed new light on a dark situation.

Joseph's Strengths and Accomplishments

- Rose to power from slave to ruler of Egypt.
- He is known for his personal integrity.
- He was a man of spiritual sensitivity.
- He prepared a nation to survive a famine.

Joesph's Weakness and Mistake

- His youthful pride caused friction with his brothers.

Lessons from Joeseph's Life

- What matters the most is not so much the events or circumstances of life, but your response to them.
- With God's help, any situation can be used for good, even when others intend it for evil.

Vital Statistics

- WHERE: Canaan and Egypt
- OCCUPATION: Shepherd, slave, convict, and ruler
- RELATIVES: Parents ➔ Jacob + Rachel
    - ½ brothers ➔ Reuben + Simeon + Levi + Judah + Issachar
                Zebulun + Gad + Asher + Dan + Naphtali
    - Full brother ➔ Benjamin
    - ½ sister ➔ Dinah
    - Wife ➔ Asenath
    - Sons ➔ Manasseh + Ephraim

THE BOOK OF GENESIS
CHAPTERS 37-50
THE STORY OF JOSEPH

THE STORY OF JOSEPH ... (37:1—50:26)

Joseph, one of Jacob's 12 sons, was obviously the favorite. Hated by his brothers for this, Joesph was sold to slave traders only to emerge as ruler of all Egypt. Through Joseph, we learn how suffering, no matter how unfair, develops strong character and deep wisdom.

(37:3) ... In Joseph's day, everyone had a coat, or cloak. Cloaks were used for warmth, to bundle up belongings for a trip, to wrap babies, to sit on, or security for a loan. Joseph's coat was probably the kind worn by royalty: long-sleeved, ankle length, and colorful. It became a symbol of Jacob's favoritism towards Joseph, it aggravated the already strained relationship with Joseph's brothers. Parents may not be able to change their feelings toward a favorite child, but they can change their actions towards others.

(37:6—11) … Joseph's brothers were already angry over the possibility of being ruled by their little brother. Joseph then fueled the fire with his immature attitude and boastful manner. No one enjoys a bragger. Joseph learns this the hard way. His brothers sold him into slavery to get rid of him. After several years of hardship, Joseph learned an important lesson: Since our knowledge and talents comes from God, we should thank him for them and not to brag about them (41:16).

(37:19,20) … 10 men were willing to kill their brother over a coat and his dreams. There deep jealousy grew into ugly rage, blinding them from what is right. Jealousy can be hard to recognize, because our reason for it seems to make sense. But left unchecked, jealousy can grow quickly and leads to serious sins. The longer you cultivate jealous feelings, the harder it is to uproot them. The time to deal with jealousy is when you notice yourself keeping score of what others have.

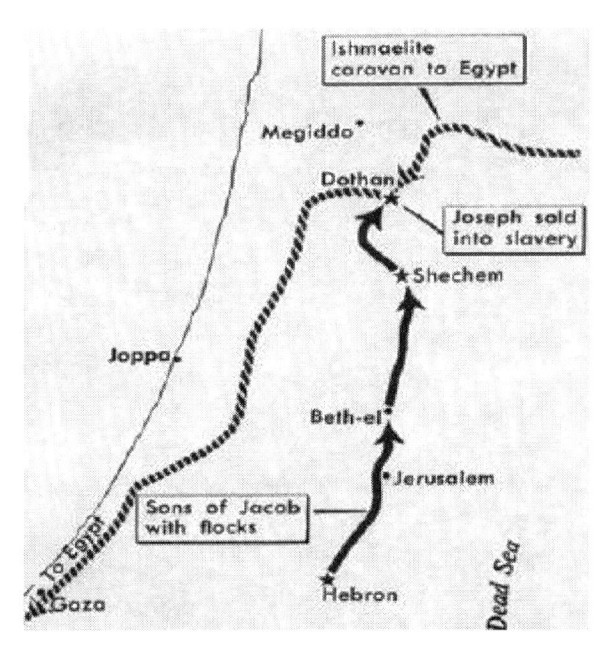

Jacob asked Joseph to go find his brothers, who were grazing their flocks near Shechem. When Joseph arrived, he learned his brothers had gone on to Dothan, which lay along a major trade route to Egypt. There the jealous brothers sold Joseph as a slave to a group of Ishmaelites traders on their way to Egypt.

(37:26,27) ... The brothers were worried about bearing the guilt of Joseph's death. Judah suggested an option that was not upright, but would leave them guiltless of murder. Sometimes we jump at a solution, because it is the lesser of 2 evils, but still isn't right. When someone proposes a workable solution, 1st ask "is it right?"

(37:28) ... Even though Joseph's brothers didn't kill him, they most likely didn't expect him to survive for long as a slave. They were willing to let cruel slave traders do their dirty work. Joseph faced 30-day journey through the desert, probably roped and on foot. He would be treated like baggage, and once in Egypt, would be sold as a piece of merchandise. His brother's thought they would never see him again.

Acts 7:9 ... And the patriarchs, moved with envy, sold Joseph into Egypt: but God was with him

(37:30) ... Reuben returned to the pit to find Joesph, but he was gone. His response was "What is going to happen to me?" (Whither shall I go?) instead of "What is going to happen to Joesph?" If you consider the person more affected by the problem, you are more likely going to find a solution for it.

(37:31—35) ... Jacob's sons deceived him into thinking Joseph was dead. Jacob had deceived others many times (including his own father; 27:35). Even though, now blessed by Hod he still had to face the consequences of his sin. The consequences stayed with him for the rest of his life.

2 Sam 12:17 ... And the elders of his house arose, and went to him, to raise him up from the earth: but he would not, neither did he eat bread with them.

Ps 77:2 ... In the day of my trouble, I sought the Lord: my sore ran in the night, and ceased not: my soul refused to be comforted.

(37:36) ... Joseph most likely experienced culture shock. Joseph lived as a nomad, traveling the countryside with his family, caring for the sheep. Suddenly, he is thrown in a world with advanced civilization, pyramids, beautiful homes, sophisticated people, and a new language. He also saw their spiritual blindness. They worshipped many gods related to every aspect of life.

JUDAH

People who are leaders stand out. They don't necessarily look or act a certain way until the need for their action is apparent. Among their skills is outspokenness, decisiveness, action, and control. These skills can be used for great good or great evil. Jacob's 4th son Judah, was a natural leader. Judah's decisions were often shaped more by pressures of the moment than by a conscious desire to cooperate with God's plan. When he did recognize his mistakes, he was willing to admit them. His experience with Tamar and the final conversation with Joseph are both examples of Judah's willingness to bear the blame, when confronted. It was one of the qualities he passed on to his descendant David.

From Judah we can learn that it is not wise to wait until our errors force us to admit to wrongdoing. It is far better to admit our mistakes openly, to shoulder the blame, and to seek forgiveness.

Judah's Strengths and Accomplishments

- Was a natural leader—outspoken and decisive.
- Thought clearly and took action in high-pressure situations.
- Was willing to put himself on the line, standing by his word
- Was the 4th son of 12, through whom God would eventually bring David and Jesus-the Messiah.

Judah's Weaknesses and Mistakes

- Suggested to his brothers that they should sell Joseph into slavery
- Failed to keep his promise to his daughter-in-law, Tamar

Lessons from Judah's Life

- God is in control, far beyond the immediate situation.
- Procrastination often makes matters worse.
- Judah's offer to substitute his life for Benjamin's is a picture of what his descendant Jesus would do for all people

Vital Statistics

- WHERE: Canaan and Egypt
- OCCUPATION: Shepherd
- RELATIVES: Parents ➔ Jacob and Leah
    Wife ➔ daughter of Shuah
    Daughter-in-law ➔ Tamar
    Brothers ➔ Reuben + Simeon + Levi + Judah + Issachar
        Zebulun + Gad + Asher + Dan + Naphtali + Benjamin
    Sister ➔ Dinah
    Sons ➔ Er + Onan + Shelah + Perez + Zerah

GENESIS

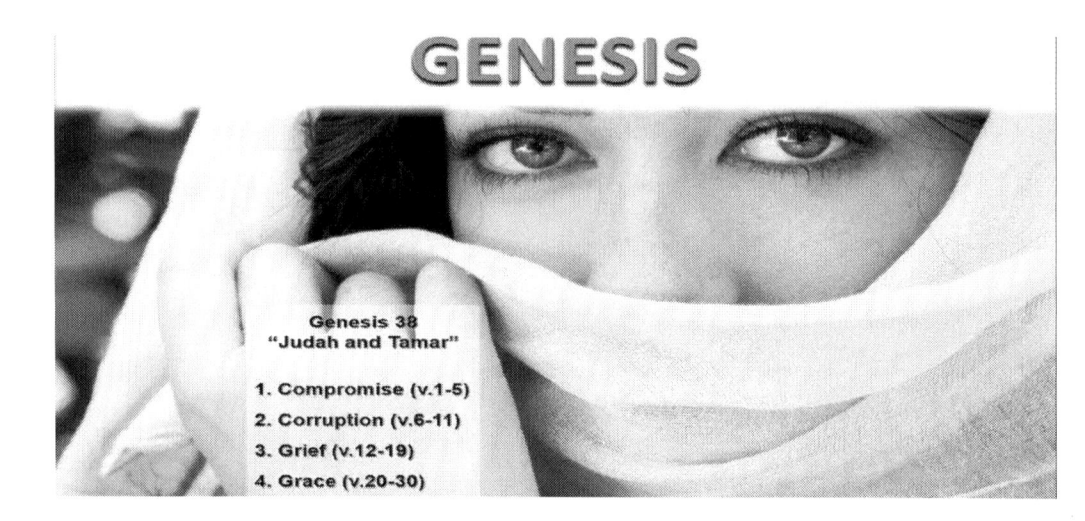

Genesis 38
"Judah and Tamar"

1. Compromise (v.1-5)
2. Corruption (v.6-11)
3. Grief (v.12-19)
4. Grace (v.20-30)

(38:1) ... This chapter portrays the immoral character of Judah in contrast to the moral character of Joseph. Judah's lack of integrity resulted in family strife and deception. In chapter 39, we see Joseph's godliness. His faithfulness was rewarded with blessings greater than he could imagine, for him and his family.

(38:8—10) ... In Deut 25:5—10, explains the law about marring a widow. Purpose was to ensure childless widows would have a son, who would receive the late husband's inheritance and who would care for her. Because Judah's son (Tamar's husband) had no children, there was no family for the inheritance could go to. God killed Onan because he refused to fulfill his obligation to his brother and Tamar.

    Matt 22:24 ... Saying, Master, Moses said, If a man die, having no children, his brother shall marry his wife, and raise up seed unto his brother.

    Mark 12:19 ... Master, Moses wrote unto us, If a man's brother die, and leave his wife behind him, and leave no children, that his brother should take his wife, and raise up seed unto his brother

(38:11-26) ... When Tamar revealed that she was pregnant, Judah, who unknowingly got her pregnant, moved to have her killed. Judah hid his own sin, but came down harshly on Tamar. Often the sins we cover up are the same ones that anger us in others. When we admit our sin and ask God to forgive us, forgiving others is easier.

Prostitution was common in heathen cultures such as Canaan. Public prostitution served heathen goddesses and were common elements of the religious cults. They were more respected than private prostitutes, who sometimes were punished when caught. Tamar was driven to seduce Judah because her desire to have children in Judah's family line and Judah was driven by lust, neither was justified.

Judah was open with his relations with a harlot, but wanted to kill his daughter-in-law for being one. A woman's most important function was bearing children who could continue the family line. The bride is expected to be a virgin, to ensure the kids belong to him. If a wife commits adultery, she could be killed. Some woman did not belong to a family and might be temple prostitutes supported by offerings or common harlots supported by the men who used their services. Their kids were not in any family line.

Judah saw no harm in hiring a harlot for a night, he was more than willing to pay. He was quick to execute Tamar, because if she was pregnant "by whoredom" his grandchild would not be from the family line.

The story in no way implies that God winks at prostitution. Throughout scripture "harlotry" is a condemned sin. If the story has a moral, it is that faithfulness to family obligations is important. Incidentally, Judah and Tamar were direct ancestors of Jesus.

JUDAH AND TAMAR FAMILY TREE

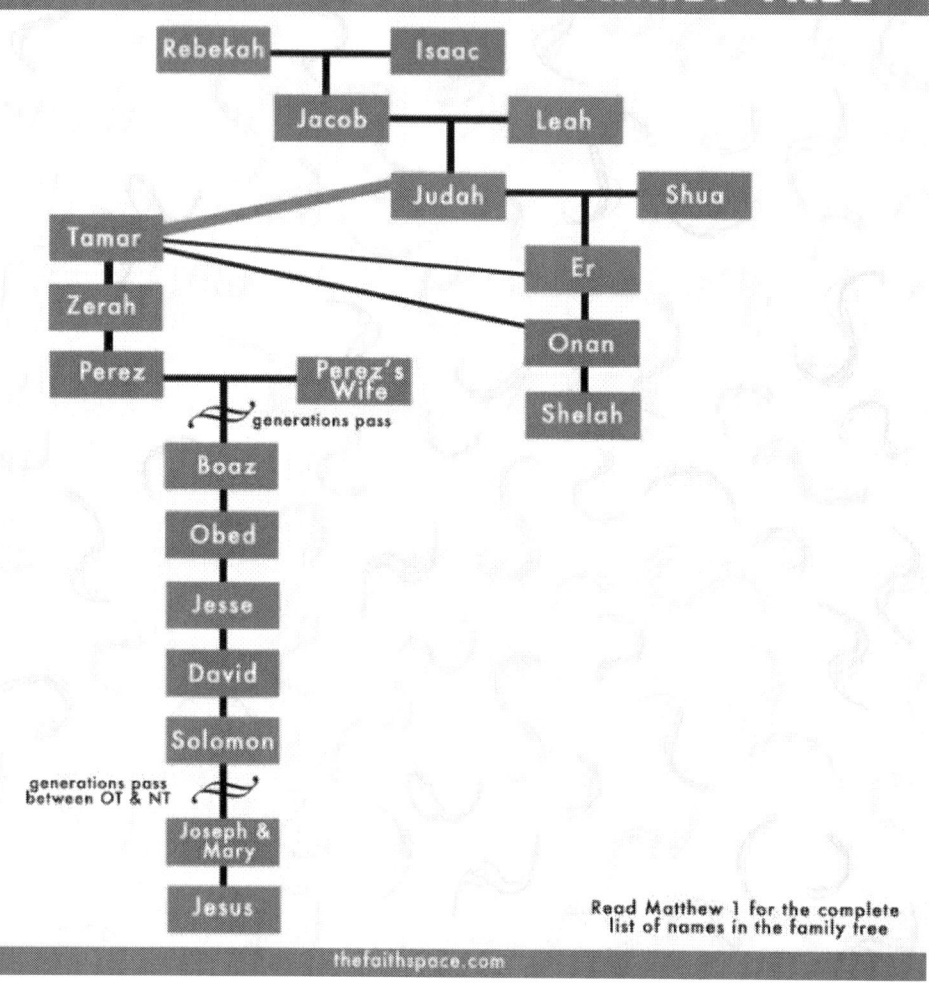

- Rebekah — Isaac
- Jacob — Leah
- Judah — Shua
- Tamar
- Er
- Onan
- Shelah
- Zerah
- Perez — Perez's Wife
- *generations pass*
- Boaz
- Obed
- Jesse
- David
- Solomon
- *generations pass between OT & NT*
- Joseph & Mary
- Jesus

Read Matthew 1 for the complete list of names in the family tree

thefaithspace.com

Women in Jesus' Family Tree

Tamar ---------- Canaanite ------------- Genesis 38:1—30

Rahab ---------- Canaanite ------------- Joshua 6:22—25

Ruth ------------ Moabite --------------- Ruth 4:13—22

Bath-Sheba -------------Israelite ---------------- 2 Samuel 12:24,35

POTIPHAR & HIS WIFE

Potiphar, captain of Pharaoh's royal guard, had a large household and a wife with too much time on her hands. Potiphar purchased Joseph from an Ishmaelite slave trader and put him to work in his home. This was the best decision Potiphar made, not only was Joseph talented, but God was with him. Because of Joseph, Potiphar prospered greatly.

Potiphar's wife started noticing Joseph's good looks. She tried to seduce him, but he continually resisted her advances. Potiphar's wife became hurt and angry. After another failed attempt, she accused Joseph of rape.

Potiphar had Joseph thrown in prison. Because he listened to a faithless woman, Potiphar jailed an innocent man and got rid of the best overseer in all Egypt. Perhaps he seen Joseph's character but didn't have enough himself to face the truth. In any case Potiphar and his wife deserved each other.

Potiphar and his wife show us that anyone can be a judge of talent, but it takes insight and courage to be a judge of character.

Potiphar and his wife's Strength's and Accomplishments

- Potiphar reached a high rank in Pharoh's court.
- They enjoyed the temporary blessing of having Joseph, God's servant, as their slave.

Potiphar and his wife's Weakness and Mistakes

- Neither recognized the amazing person who lived in their house.
- Both failed to judge character—Potiphar towards his wife and Joseph, his wife toward Joseph.
- Falsely accused and imprisoned Joseph, their faithful servant.

Lessons learned from Potiphar and his wife's Life

- A lasting marriage requires faithfulness and hard work
- God can accomplish his purpose through other's mistakes and sins
- God blesses people who clearly don't deserve his grace and help
- One person's character stands out among those who possess little of it.

Vital Statistics

- WHERE: Egypt
- OCCUPATION: Palace official and wife

(38:18) ... A signet was a form of identification used to authenticate legal documents. Usually, a unique design carved in stone and worn on a ring or necklace. Inseparable from the owner, it was used by the wealthy and powerful to mark clay or wax. Since Tamar had Judah's seal, she proved beyond a doubt he was with her.

(39:1) ... Pharaoh was the general name for all kings in Egypt. Like, in USA, we say Mr. President. It's a title for the leader. In ancient Egypt people were either rich or poor, there was no middle class. Joseph served Potiphar, a rich officer of Pharaoh, rich families like him would have large 2-3 story houses. With balconies, they had very expensive things and food was served on golden tableware. Servants like Joseph would have worked on the lower floors, while the family occupied the upper stories.

(39:9—15) ... Potiphar's wife failed to seduce Joseph, who resisted this temptation by saying it would be a sin against God. Remember that sexual sin is not just between 2 adults. It is an act of disobedience to God.

Joseph avoided Potiphar's wife as much as possible. He refused her advances and finally ran from her. We must turn and run, especially when the temptations seem very strong, as is often the case in sexual temptations.

(39:20—23) ... Prisons were grim places with vile conditions. They were used to house forced laborers, or like Joseph, the accused awaiting trial. Many prisoners never made it to court, for trials were held at the whim of the ruler. Joseph was in prison a long time before going before Pharaoh, and then it was to interpret dream, not stand trial. As a prisoner and slave, Joseph could have seen his situation as hopeless, instead; he did his best with each small task given him. His diligence and positive attitude were soon noticed by the warden, who promoted him to prison administer. Remember how God turned Joseph's situation around. He will see your efforts and can reverse even overwhelming odds.

The Butler and the Baker
Genesis 40

(40:1—3) ... The butler and baker were 2 of the most trusted men in Pharaoh's kingdom. The baker was in charge of making the king's food, and the butler tasted all the king's food and drink before giving it to him, in case any was poisoned. These men must have been suspected of serious wrong. Later the butler was released and the baker executed.

(40:8) ... When the subject of dreams came up, Joseph focused everyone's attention on God. He turned this into a powerful witness for God. One secret of effective witnessing is to recognize opportunities to relate God to others personal experiences.

    Daniel 2:27—28) ... Daniel answered in the presence of the king, and said, the secret which the king hath demanded cannot the wise men, the astrologers, the magicians, the soothsayers, shew unto the king; But there is a God in heaven that revealeth secrets, and maketh known to the king Nebuchadnezzar what shall be in the latter days. Thy dream, and the visions of thy head upon thy bed, are these;

The Butler's Dream:
3 Vines = 3 Days

The Chief Baker's Dream:
3 Baskets = 3 Days

(40:23) ... When Pharaoh's butler was freed from prison, he forgot about Joseph, even though he had Joseph to thank for his freedom. It was 2 full years before Joseph had another opportunity to be freed (41:1). Joseph's faith was deep, and he would be ready when the next chance came. When we feel overlooked or forgotten, we shouldn't be surprised that people are often ungrateful. In situations like this, trust God. Like Joseph. More opportunities maybe waiting.

PHARAOH'S DREAMS

(41:8) ... Magicians and wise men were common in the palaces of ancient rulers. Their job description included studying sacred arts and sciences, reading the starts, interpreting dreams, predicting the future, and performing magic. These men had power (Ex 7:11-12), but their power was satanic.

>Daniel 2:1—3 ... And in the second year of the reign of Nebuchadnezzar, Nebuchadnezzar dreamed dreams, wherewith his spirit was troubled, and his sleep brake from him. Then the king commanded to call the magicians, and the astrologers, and the sorcerers, and the Chaldeans, for to shew the king his dreams. So, they came and stood before the king. And the king said unto them, I have dreamed a dream, and my spirit was troubled to know the dream.

(41:14) ... Our most important opportunities may come when we least expect them. Joseph was brought from the dungeon and put before Pharaoh. He had no warning that he would go before Pharaoh and be questioned. Yet Joseph was ready because is relationship with God. His knowledge of God helped him interpret the dream. Be ready for opportunities by getting to know God more.

>Ps 105:20 ... The king sent and loosed him; even the ruler of the people, and let him go free.

(41:28—36) ... After interpreting Pharaoh's dream, Joseph gave the king a survival plan for the next 14 years. The only way to prevent starvation was through careful planning; without "Famine plan" Egypt would have turned from might to ruin. Planning is a responsibility not an option. We must take time to translate God's plan for us into practical actions.

(41:38) ... Pharoah recognized that Joseph was a man "in whom the Spirit of God is". People should be able to see God in you, through your words, acts, and wise advice. Do others see this in you?

    Daniel 5:14 ... I have even heard of thee, that the spirit of the gods is in thee, and that light and understanding and excellent wisdom is found in thee.

(41:39,40) ... Joseph rose quickly to the top, from prison walls to pharaoh's palace. His training involved being 1st a slave then prisoner. In both situations he learned importance of serving God and others. No matter your situation, consider it part of your training program for serving God.

Ps 105:21 ... He made him lord of his house, and ruler of all his substance:

Acts 7:10 ... And delivered him out of all his afflictions, and gave him favour and wisdom in the sight of Pharaoh king of Egypt; and he made him governor over Egypt and all his house.

(41:45) ... Pharah may have been trying to acculturate Joesph by giving him an Egyptian name "Zaphnath-Paaneah" and an Egyptian wife named Asenath.

He probably wanted to:

1. Play down that Joseph was a nomad shepherd.
2. A name easier for Egyptians to pronounce and remember.
3. Show how honored he was by giving him the daughter of a prominent Egyptian official.

(41:46) ... Joseph was 30 years old when he became governor of Egypt. He was 17 years old when he was sold into slavery. Thus, he spent 13 years as a slave and in prison.

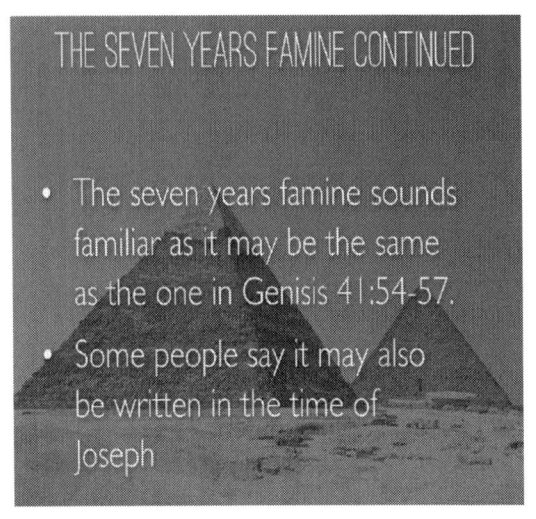

THE SEVEN YEARS FAMINE CONTINUED

- The seven years famine sounds familiar as it may be the same as the one in Genisis 41:54-57.
- Some people say it may also be written in the time of Joseph

(41:54) ... Famine was a catastrophe in antient times. Almost perfect conditions were needed to produce good crops, because there were no fertilization or pesticides. Any variance in rainfall or insect activity could cause crop failure and great hunger. Lack of storage, refrigeration, or transportation turned a moderate famine into a desperation. Without God's intervention the Egyptian nation would have crumbled.

Acts 7:11 ... Now there came a dearth over all the land of Egypt and Chanaan, and great affliction: and our fathers found no sustenance.

(42:1,2) ... Corn and grain was so valuable because it was used in nearly everything eaten. It could be dried and stored longer than other vegetables, milk products, or meat. It was so important it was often used as money.

Acts 7:12 ... But when Jacob heard that there was corn in Egypt, he sent out our fathers first.

(42:4) ... Jacob was especially fond of Benjamin because he was Joseph's only full brother and -as far as Jacob knew- the only surviving son of his beloved wife, Rachel.

(42:7-9) ... Joseph could have revealed his identity to his brothers at once, but his last memory was starring, in horror, at their faces as slave traders carried him away. Joseph decided to put them to the test to see if they had changed.

Joseph remembered the dream he had about his brothers. As a young boy he was boastful; but as a man he no longer flaunted his superior status. It was not time to reveal his identity, so he kept quiet. Sometimes its best to keep quite when we would love to have the last word.

(42:15) ... Joseph was testing his brothers to make sure they had not been cruel to Benjamin, as they did him. Benjamin was his only full brother and he wanted to see him face to face.

The Second Journey To Egypt
GENESIS 43:1-34

(43:1) ... Jacob and his sons had no relief from the famine. They could not see God's overall plan, of sending them to Egypt to be reunited with Joesph, and fed from the Egyptian storehouses. If you are praying for relief from suffering or pressure and God is not bringing it as quickly as you would like, remember that God maybe lending you to special treasure.

(43:9) ... Judah accepted full responsibility for Benjamin's safety. He did not know what that might mean for him, but he was determined to do his duty. Accepting responsibility is difficult, but it builds character and confidence, earns others' respect, and motivates is to complete our work.

    Phil 1:18—19 ... If he hath wronged thee, or oweth thee ought, put that on mine account; I Paul have written it with mine own hand, I will repay it: albeit I do not say to thee how thou owest unto me even thine own self besides.

(43:11) ... These gifts of balm, honey, and spices, myrrh, nuts, and almonds were highly valuable specialty items not common in Egypt. Because of the famine, they were even more rare.

(43:12) ... Joesph's brothers arrive home from Egypt only to find in their grain sacks the money they had used to pay for the grain (42:35). Some months later when it was time to return to Egypt for more food, Jacob told them to take extra money so they could pay for the previous food they got. He was a man of integrity. A reputation for honesty is worth far more than money we might gain by compromising it.

(43:32) ... Joesph ate by himself, because he was following the laws of the Egyptians' caste system. Egyptians looked upon shepherds and nomads as uncultured and even vulgar.

<u>Exodus 8:26</u> ... And Moses said, It is not meet so to do; for we shall sacrifice the abomination of the Egyptians to the LORD our God: lo, shall we sacrifice the abomination of the Egyptians before their eyes, and will they not stone us?

JOSEPH & THE SILVER CUP

& God's Saving Power!

(44:2) ... Joseph's silver cup was a symbol of his authority. It was thought to have supernatural powers and to steal it was a serious crime. Such goblets were used to predict the future. A person poured water into a cup and interpret the reflections, ripples, and bubbles. Joseph didn't need the cup, God told him everything he needed to know about the future.

(44:13) ... Rending and ripping clothes was an expression of deep sorrow, a customary manner of showing grief. The brothers were terrified that Benjamin might be harmed.

(44:16—34) ... When Judah was younger, he showed no regard for his brother Joseph or his father, Jacob. 1st he convinced his brothers to sell Joseph as a slave (37:27); then he joined his brothers in lying to his father about Joseph's fate (37:32). What a change had taken place in Judah! The man who sold 1 favored little brother into slavery now offered to become a slave himself to save another favored little brother.

(44:32,33) ... Judah had promised Jacob he would guarantee young Benjamin's safety (43:9). Now Judah had a chance to keep that promise. Accepting a responsibility with determination and courage, regardless of the personal sacrifice.

Joesph wanted to see if his brothers' attitudes had changed for the better, so he tested the way they treated each other. Judah, the brother to step forward with plan the plan to sell Joseph (37:27) now stepped up to take Benjamin's punishment so Benjamin could return to the father. That's courage!

(45:4—8) ... Although Joesph's brothers wanted to get rid of him, God used their evil actions to fulfill his ultimate plan. He sent Joseph ahead to [reserve their lives, save Egypt, and prepare the way for the beginning of the nation of Israel. When others intend evil on you, remember they are only God's tools. As Joesph said to his brothers, "Ye thought evil against me; but God meant it unto good"

(45:17—20) ... Joseph was rejected, kidnapped, enslaved, and imprisoned. Although his brothers had been unfaithful to him, he graciously forgave them and shared his prosperity. Joesph demonstrated how God forgives us and showers us with goodness even though we sin against him.

(45:26,27) ... Jacob needed proof that Joesph was alive. Similarly, Thomas refused to believe Jesus rose from the dead unless he had proof (John 20:25). Good news can be hard to believe. Don't give up hope that God has wonderful things in store for you.

(46:3,4) ... The Israelites did become a great nation, and Jacob's descendants eventually returned to Canaan, Exodus will recount Israel's slavery in Egypt for 400 years and in Joshua gives an exciting account of Israel entering and conquering Canaan, the Promised Land.

    God told Jacob to leave his home and travel to a strange and faraway land. God promised to be with and care for him. To be paralyzed by fear is an indication that you question God's ability to take care of you.

    Jacob never returned to Canaan. It was promised that his descendants would return. "Joesph shall put his hand upon thine eyes" refers to attending to him as he faced death.

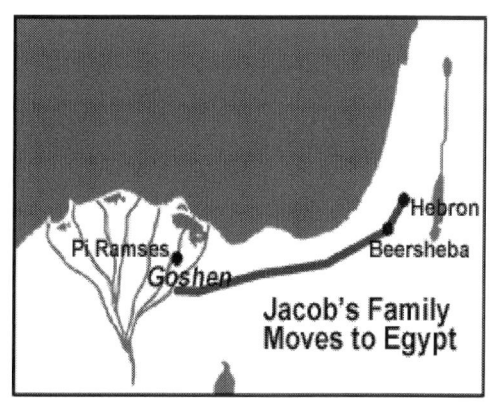

After hearing the joyful news that Joseph was alive, Jacob packed up and moved his family to Egypt. Stopping 1st in Beer-Sheba Jacob offered sacrifices and received assurance from God that Egypt was where he should go. Jacob and his family settled in the land of Goshen, in northeast Egypt.

Jacob's Family Moves to Egypt

(46:31—34) ... Jacob moved his family to Egypt but wanted to live apart from the Egyptians. Although Pharaoh may have been sympathetic to shepherds (for he was probably descended from the nomadic Hyksos line) the Egyptian culture would not willingly accept shepherds in their midst. The strategy worked; Jacob's family was able to benefit from the Pharoah's generosity as well as from the Egyptians prejudice.

(47:1—6) ... The faithfulness of Joesph affected his entire family. We may not always see the effects of our faith, but we can be sure that God will honor our faithfulness.

(47:29—31) ... Jacob has Joesph's promise to bury him in his homeland. God's people are to speak and live the truth. Let your words be as binding as a written contract.

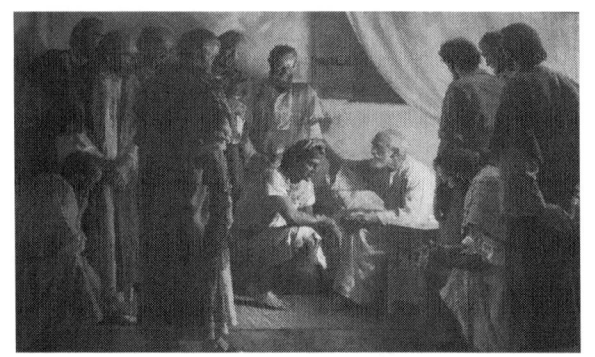

(48:8—22) ... Jacob gave Ephraim, instead of his older brother Manasseh, the greater blessing. When Joesph objected, Jacob refused to listen, for God told him Ephraim would become greater.

When Joesph became a slave, Jacob thought he would never see him again. Not only did he regain his son but his grandchildren as well. Circumstances are never so bad that they are beyond God's help. Jacob talked about God as one who fed him his whole life. In his old age, he could see clearly his independence on God. This is a total change from his scheming youth. To develop an attitude like Jacob's be willing to be fed. Jacob was giving these young bots land occupied by the Philistines and Canaanites. His gift became a reality when the tribes of Ephraim and Manasseh occupied the east and west sides of Jordan River (Joshua 16).

(49:3—28) ... Jacob blessed each son, and then made prediction about each son's future. The wat they lived had a part in Jacob's blessing and prophecy. Our past affects our present and future. By morning, our actions of today will become our past. Yet they will have begun to shape our future.

(49:4) ... Reuben, being the oldest, was suppose to receive 2x's the inheritance, but he lost this special honor.

(49:8-12) ... Even though Judah sold Joesph to slavery and tried to defraud his daughter-in-law, God chose him to be the ancestor of Israel's line of kings. Most likely to his change in character (44:33,34). Judah's line would produce the promised Messiah, Jesus. Shiloh may be another name for the Messiah, for its literal meaning is "sent". It might also refer to the tabernacle set up at the city of Shiloh (Joshua 18:1).

(49:18,22) ... He was emphasizing to Dan that he would be a strong leader only if his trust was in God, not in his natural strength or ability.

    Joesph was fruitful with some heroic descendants.

Joshua—led the Israelites into the Promised Land (Joshua 1:10,11)

Deborah & Gideon—Judges of Israel (Judges 4:4; 6:11,12)

Samuel—A great prophet (1 Samuel 3:19)

Jacob and Joseph's Death
Genesis Begins With Life But Ends in Death
Genesis Chapter 50

(50:1—13) ... When Jacob died at 147 years old, Joesph wept and mourned for months. Give yourself time to bring grieving to a completion.

Abraham had purchased the Cave of Machpelah as a burial place for his wife, Sarah. It was a burial place for the entire family. Their desire to be buried in this cave expressed their faith in God's promise to give their descendants the land of Canaan.

(50:15—24) ... Joesph not only forgave his brothers but offered to care for them and their families. He demonstrated how God graciously accepts us even though we don't deserve it.

Joesph was ready to die. He has no doubts that God would keep his promise and one day bring Israelites back to their homeland. This verse sets the stage for what would begin to happen in Exodus and come to completion in Joshua. The nation would rely heavily on the promise, and Joseph emphasized his belief that God would do what he promised.

Jacob's sons and their notable descendants

Reuben	None
Simeon	None
Levi	Aaron + Moses + Eli + John the Baptist
Judah	David + Jesus
Dan	Samson
Naphtali	Barak + Elijah (?)
Gad	Jephthah (?)
Asher	None
Issachar	None
Zebulun	None
Joseph	Joshua + Deborah + Gideon + Samuel
Benjamin	Saul + Esther + Paul

Sons of Jacob / Tribes of Israel

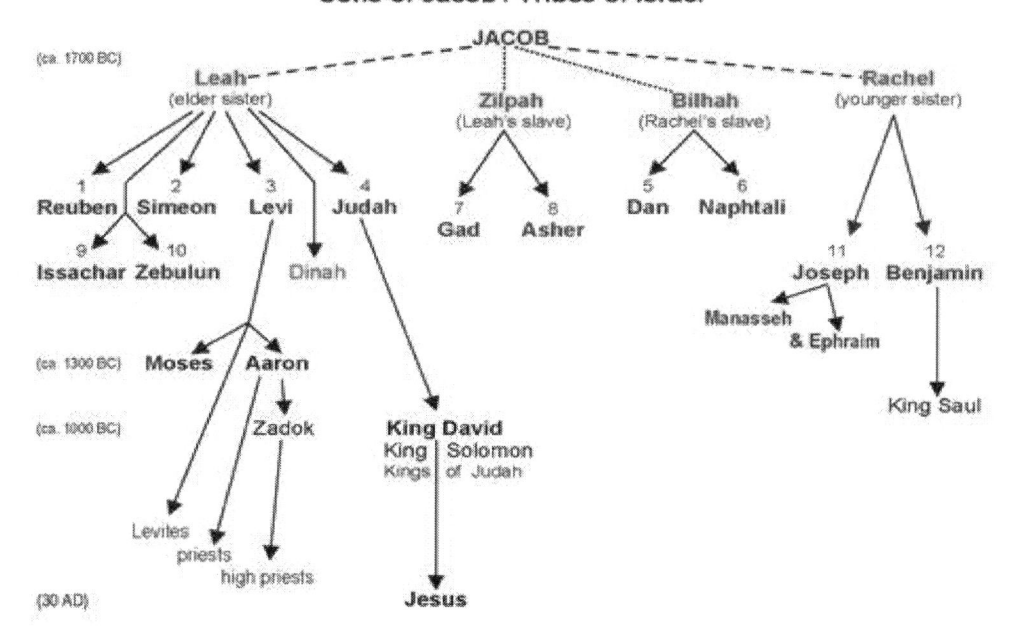

(ca. 1700 BC)

JACOB

- Leah (elder sister)
  - 1. Reuben
  - 2. Simeon
  - 3. Levi
  - 4. Judah
  - 9. Issachar
  - 10. Zebulun
  - Dinah
- Zilpah (Leah's slave)
  - 7. Gad
  - 8. Asher
- Bilhah (Rachel's slave)
  - 5. Dan
  - 6. Naphtali
- Rachel (younger sister)
  - 11. Joseph
    - Manasseh & Ephraim
  - 12. Benjamin
    - King Saul

(ca. 1300 BC) Moses / Aaron

(ca. 1000 BC) Zadok

Levites
priests
high priests

King David
King | Solomon
Kings of Judah

(30 AD) Jesus

Parallels Between Joesph and Jesus (Gen 37—50)

Joesph	Parallels	Jesus
37:3	Father loved him dearly	Matt 3:17
37:2	Shepherd of Father's sheep	John 10:11,27
37:13,14	Sent by father to brothers	Heb 2:11
37:4	Hated by brothers	John 7:5
37:20	Others plotted to harm them	John 11:53
39:7	Tempted	Matt 4:1
37:25	Taken to Egypt	Matt 2:14,15
37:23	Robes taken from them	John 19:23
37:28	Sold for price of a slave	Matt 26:15
39:20	Bound in chains	Matt 27:2
39:16—18	Falsely accused	Matt 26:59,60
40:2,3	Place with 2 prisoners 1 saved 1 lost	Luke 23:32
41:46	30 yrs. old at beginning of public ministry	Luke 3:23
41:41	Exalted after suffering	Phil 2:9—11
45:1—15	Forgave those who wronged them	Luke 23:34
45:7	Saved their nation	Matt 1:21
50:20	What men did to hurt them God turned to good.	1 Cor 2:7,8